W9-DEV-737

Angels ROUND ABOUT

True Stories of the Lord's Tender Mercies

OTHER BOOKS AND AUDIO BOOKS
BY JUDY C. OLSEN:

Beyond the Horizon

Angels ROUND ABOUT

True Stories of the Lord's Tender Mercies

compiled by Judy C. Olsen

Covenant Communications, Inc.

Cover image *Protection* © Amanda Rohde, courtesy of istockphoto.com

Cover design copyrighted 2010 by Covenant Communications, Inc.

Published by Covenant Communications, Inc.
American Fork, Utah

Copyright © 2010 by Judy C. Olsen
All rights reserved. No part of this book may be reproduced in any format or in any medium without the written permission of the publisher, Covenant Communications, Inc., P.O. Box 416, American Fork, UT 84003. This work is not an official publication of The Church of Jesus Christ of Latter-day Saints. The views expressed within this work are the sole responsibility of the author and do not necessarily reflect the position of The Church of Jesus Christ of Latter-day Saints, Covenant Communications, Inc., or any other entity.

Printed in the United States of America
First Printing: March 2010

17 16 15 14 13 12 11 10   10 9 8 7 6 5 4 3 2 1

ISBN-13: 978-1-59811-948-0

To my children and grandchildren.

May you always live up to your privilege to receive
the Lord's tender mercies in your lives.

Acknowledgments

It has been my privilege to communicate with many people as I have gathered these stories. I thank them for their willingness to share such personal experiences. Within each story can be found profound lessons that demonstrate how, under the direction of the Father and the Son and through the power of the Holy Ghost, we can be protected, inspired, converted, healed, and taught. Surely the angels are watching over us, and the Lord is pouring out His tender mercies upon us, His chosen people.

These accounts reveal some of those tender moments when Latter-day Saints experience personal evidence of the Lord's watchful care over those of us who live in this dispensation of the fulness of times. Thank you to all for sharing your stories.

Introduction

Heavenly Father loves all of His children and is mindful of each one of them. As we seek our Lord and Savior in faith, we will feel His goodness as He blesses our lives in multiple ways. We are told that the angels of heaven will be "round about you, to bear you up" (D&C 84:88). This great blessing comes to all of us who seek to follow the teachings of the Savior. And in 1 Nephi, we learn that "the tender mercies of the Lord are over all those whom he hath chosen, because of their faith, to make them mighty even unto the power of deliverance" (1 Nephi 1:20). These are profound promises to the faithful.

Elder David A. Bednar of the Quorum of the Twelve, says tender mercies are

> the very personal and individualized blessings, strength, protection, assurances, guidance, loving-kindnesses, consolation, support, and spiritual gifts which we receive from and because of and through the Lord Jesus Christ. . . .
>
> The simpleness, the sweetness, and the constancy of the tender mercies of the Lord will do much to fortify and protect us in the troubled times which we do now and will yet live. ("The Tender Mercies of the Lord," *Ensign,* May 2005, 99)

This volume contains true accounts of Latter-day Saints who have experienced the Lord's tender mercies in the midst of trying circumstances. As we read of their faith, prayers, and obedience to promptings, we can share the profound lessons and tender moments they received from the hand of a loving Father in Heaven. Assuredly, the angels are "round about" faithful Saints today.

—Judy C. Olsen

Contents

Kind Understandings

*There is no doubt, if a person lives according
to the revelations given to God's people, he may have the
Spirit of the Lord to signify to him his will, and to guide and to
direct him in the discharge of his duties, in his temporal as well as his
spiritual exercises. I am satisfied, however, that in this respect,
we live far beneath our privileges.*

*—Brigham Young,
Discourses of Brigham Young,
selected and arranged by John A. Widtsoe, 1943, 32*

Heartfelt Supplications

*Whatsoever ye shall ask in faith, being
united in prayer according to my command,
ye shall receive.*

—D&C 29:6

The Fourth-of-July Snowstorm

by Patricia Thelin and family

Patricia: While living in Washington State, we liked to hike and camp out often as a family. On the Fourth of July one year, I went camping with six of my seven children and some of their cousins at Salmon Meadows in the north-central part of the state.

My son Michael, sixteen at the time, and his cousin Roger decided to hike six miles over the top of the mountain to a lake on the other side of the mountain. He had some maps and a compass, and with his Scouting experience, I thought he would be fine. I decided to put the rest of the children into the car, drive the long way around, and wait for them near the lake on the other side.

All the younger teenagers begged to go, and while I finally told Mike and Roger okay, I hesitated to let the two girls and my young son go along. It was a long, rigorous hike that no one was familiar with.

Mike quickly drew out a rough map in case the others followed. Then the two boys took off, and I thought it was settled. But the other teenagers continued to work on me. "If they can go, why can't we? If we hurry up, we can catch up with them!"

I thought about it for a while and finally relented. Why not? So Bonnie, Donna, and Gordon ran up the trail and were soon lost from sight in the heavily wooded mountainside. No one remembered the map. Mike was at least a half hour in front of them—maybe more. Still, I told myself that if they stayed on the trail, they'd be fine.

I got into my car, along with my two younger children, and began the long drive around to the lake. As I drove the scenic miles, I noticed the weather clouding up. I eyed the mountaintop, which looked like it was covered in clouds.

Gordon: It was a very hot day, and we had been swimming in one of the lakes in the area. I had just turned twelve, and I felt I was practically grown up—not one of the babies to be left behind with Mom. After Mike left, we talked Mom into letting us catch up with him and Roger. We took off, the girls wearing T-shirts and me in shorts.

Bonnie: We were sure we would catch up with Mike and Roger in no time. Because I knew Mom was going to drive around and meet us on the other side, there was only one thing to do: find Mike! We confidently headed up the trail and soon found ourselves deep in the woods. Then we came to a fork in the trail and stopped. A trail sign had been knocked down, and we couldn't tell which way to go. I hadn't counted on there being more than one trail. As the oldest, I felt responsible. I glanced back, suddenly wishing we had stayed with Mom. But she would be gone by now. We had to keep on the trail and get over the mountain somehow.

Gordon: We searched for some sign or other marker to tell us which trail headed to the lake. After several minutes of trying to figure out which way to go, Bonnie finally gathered us around for a prayer. We had always prayed as a family, and this seemed like the best answer. We stood in a circle and folded our arms.

After the prayer, I found myself studying the footprints trampled into the dirt on both trails—there were many in both directions. Suddenly, I recognized something familiar. I pointed to one set and said, "Those are Mike's prints—I'm sure of it!"

Everyone agreed. We knew which way to go! I realized my eyes had been helped to "see" after we had sincerely asked for help. I felt a deep gratitude inside. In fact, we all felt such gratitude that we stopped again and said a prayer of thanks. Then we hurried up the trail, confident that our challenges were over.

But we were wrong. Soon we came to another fork in the trail. This was going to be harder than we thought. But this time, knowing what to look for, I confidently searched for Mike's shoe prints. But I couldn't see anything special. Disappointed, we were quicker to try prayer.

As I said my little prayer, a strong feeling came to me for which way to go. But . . . would my older sisters feel that way? When we were done praying, we discovered that *we had all been given the same answer!* Each of us had experienced an understanding of which way to go.

Feeling even more gratitude, if that were possible, we bowed our heads, and again we offered a prayer of thanks.

The weather was clouding up, and the higher we went, the colder it became. Then, much to our consternation, it began to snow—on the Fourth of July! It snowed so hard that within minutes the trail was completely obliterated. I shivered, feeling extremely cold. We had no coats or sweaters with us.

The trail, which was not heavily used, had been difficult to follow anyway, and now it had all but disappeared. As we continued, our prayers took on increasing urgency, and we stopped frequently to pray to know where to go. At one point, it was snowing so hard we had to hold onto one another so as not to lose each other in the snowstorm. If only we could find Mike.

Mike: My cousin Roger and I had a good time hiking through the woods—for a while, anyway. With the help of the maps, a compass, and an altimeter, we quickly moved along the trail. After a few miles, we came to a triple fork in the trail. There were quite a few paths leading to other lakes and mountaintops along the trail. We located the correct branch to take and continued on.

After about half a mile, I felt very strongly that I should go back and mark the right path, as we had been taught to do in Scouts. I told Roger what I felt, even though it meant backtracking. Still, it had been such a strong feeling that we decided to turn back and leave a marker.

When we reached the fork in the trail, we set four rocks on top of each other, the top one pointing to the correct trail. Then we retraced our footsteps. After a while, we came across another fork. The trail had leveled out by now. We soon came to some meadows. This time we knew right away that we needed to mark the path. We did not know why, but we continued to feel strongly that we needed to mark the direction to go.

As we went along, we noticed it was getting colder—a lot colder. Then it started to snow! So we hurried even faster. The trail was very shallow and hard to see for the last two miles. With the map and altimeter I'd brought along, I was able to figure out the correct path, but I knew that anyone without a map would not be able to stay on the right trail. So we continued to place trail markers on our way to the lake.

Patricia: I arrived at the lake and parked, straining to see through the swirling snow. I expected my children to come running along the trail to the lakeside any minute. But I couldn't see anyone coming off the mountain. Time passed, and I began to worry. None of them had coats, and I worried that they were freezing cold and wet. Would they be lost in the storm? I prayed for them. I debated whether to look for them or to go for help. But if I left, they might get here and find me gone, along with warmth and coats. My anxiety increased, and so did my pleadings in prayer for their safety.

Finally, I saw movement on the trail. Relieved, I waved them over. Mike and Roger got to the car, cold, exhausted, and shivering. As they climbed in, I asked them, "Where are the others?"

"Did they follow us?" my son asked. "We never saw them!"

Apprehension formed a pit in my stomach. At that point, I began to panic. My eyes flew back to the trail, hoping to see the others emerge. But it remained empty. "They started up behind you a while after you left. You never saw them?"

Mike shook his head. "No, and the trail is very hard to follow. Did they take the map I drew?"

"No, they forgot it. I'd better go find them. Hand me their coats. I'm going to hike up to meet them. You two stay with the younger ones."

"Mom, I placed markers along the last couple of miles."

I just looked at my son and then turned to look at the trail. Doubts assailed me.

"Just follow the markers. They'll take you up the right trail."

I piled the coats over my arm and headed up the track. The *right* trail? *How many trails were there?* My concern deepened as I hurried along.

Just as he said, I found trail markers from time to time and was able to follow them at every turn. As I climbed, the great blessing of having the markers to guide me became more and more evident. After a while, I came out of the woods to find a huge meadow covered in snow. Not a footprint could be seen. No trail markers could be seen. I didn't know which way to cross. I began to shout my children's names.

Bonnie: I knew we were in trouble. The snow made it hard to know where to go. But I felt the Spirit guiding us—all of us—and that gave me hope. As we hurried along the trail, we stopped each time we needed direction and offered prayers. Each time we would all receive an impression of the direction we should go. And each time we offered prayers of gratitude before moving on. This "witness" to each of us was important because we were in perfect agreement and able to move more quickly along the right path.

As the snow deepened, it covered any sign of a trail. We stopped. The woods had finally thinned out, and we found ourselves standing by the edge of what was probably a meadow that stretched away in front of us, but the snow came down so heavily that we couldn't guess which way to go. There was no trail, no landmarks, no indication of a path. The kinds of impressions we had been receiving up to this time would no longer serve. In the swirling snow, we wouldn't even know which direction we were heading. We were lost. We were freezing cold in the snow, and we were in serious trouble.

Shivering and desperate, we decided this time we would kneel down in the snow to pray.

Gordon: As I ended my prayer, I had faith that Heavenly Father would help us because I had felt so much guidance to this point. So I stayed on my knees in the snow, waiting for inspiration to come. But nothing came to mind.

Instead, a beautiful sound interrupted my prayerful meditation—my mom's voice calling to us! I jumped up and realized that it was coming from the other side of a small rise in the meadow.

Bonnie: We took off running, hollering, "Mom! We're here!" Following the sounds of our voices, we soon found each other. What a joyful reunion. Relief flooded through me.

We gratefully put on our coats and offered another prayer of gratitude. But when we turned to go, we realized the snow was coming down so hard that even my mom's recent footprints had been covered. We were still lost in the snowstorm!

"Come on, kids," said Mom. "I know there's a trail marker on the other side of the meadow. It will point the way to go. We'll walk around the edge of the meadow until we find it."

It was a long walk, but at last we found the marker, and we were able to hike to the car in safety. Our brother's obedience in listening to the Spirit and placing the markers on the last part of the trail truly made it possible for us to get down the mountain safely. We were so grateful to see our car and to know that we were going to be okay. And we knew that each of us, in a very personal way, had received special guidance that day.

We learned, in a way we had never before appreciated, that Heavenly Father is aware of us. He had heard our prayers and brought us to safety. The remarkable guidance each of us received—Mike to mark the last part of the trail and the three of us each receiving personal witnesses of which direction to take at every fork in the road—left a deep impression on our young minds. We all gained testimonies that have never left us of the love and concern our Father in Heaven has for us.

I came away with a deep feeling of how special my family is and how much I love them.

Gordon: Two months later I attended my first Scout camp. The first day of camp was Sunday, and the Latter-day Saint Scouts met together in a fast and testimony meeting in an outdoor amphitheater. I got up and told this story. As I shared my experience, the Spirit bore witness to me of the truthfulness of the gospel. I began to cry as I realized that not only does our Heavenly Father answer prayer, but also that everything I had been taught about Joseph Smith, the Book of Mormon, the Atonement . . . it was all true. Our adventure in the woods on that Fourth of July led to the testimony that I still have today.

Patricia Thelin is a mother of seven, grandmother of thirty-seven, and great-grandmother of twelve. She loves to read, crochet, and go camping, especially with her family.

Michael Thelin, father of six and grandfather of five, lives in Pleasant Grove, Utah, with his wife, Sherilynn.

Bonnie Smith, mother of five, lives in Kennewick, Washington. The family enjoys camping, swimming, dancing, and playing games together.

Gordon Thelin, father of five, lives in rural Virginia near the Blue Ridge Mountains, where he likes to take his family hiking, camping, and skiing.

Trust in the Lord with all thine heart;
and lean not unto thine own understanding.
In all thy ways acknowledge him, and
he shall direct thy paths.

—Proverbs 3:5–6

Two Sick Babies—A Generation Apart

by Beth Shumway Moore

Iwas very blessed to be born of "goodly parents" (1 Nephi 1:1) who taught me many righteous principles and did their best to set a good example. One teaching I particularly remember is the miraculous power of the Holy Ghost, whose still, small voice, under the direction of our Savior, warns, cautions, inspires, and communicates love for us. From my parents, I also learned about the power of the priesthood as they recounted my own "miracle" of healing.

In 1928 when I was ten months old, I was stricken with polio, and my legs were paralyzed. Polio was a terrifying disease at that time, and a small epidemic hit our little Wyoming town. My mother was a registered nurse and was familiar with the disease. At the time, the common practice for treating polio was to put the afflicted limbs in cement casts. My mother thought that was the worst thing that could be done.

At first Mother didn't tell Father that I had polio. He had a sister who'd been left partially paralyzed by polio, and if he'd realized that was why I was so slow to walk, he'd have insisted on taking me to specialists. Mother didn't want that. Those were Depression years, and there wasn't much money. And besides, as a nurse she knew there was little they could do. Instead, she prayed constantly, and during those early months of my life, she felt the Lord gave answers to her prayers through ideas and impressions that came to mind. She exercised and massaged my legs with tears on a daily basis.

My father, knowing only that I was ill, gave me many priesthood blessings during my first year of life. When I was about eighteen months old, I finally learned to walk. This was a great miracle that few understood at the time. But my mother, especially, realized that I had been greatly blessed.

My legs have always been the weak link in my body, but I have lived a full and, I hope, productive life. Now as I age, I suffer from leg fatigue and some pain. I do my part in eating healthy, keeping my weight down, and getting enough rest. In addition, priesthood blessings through the years have helped me maintain wonderful health. The story of faith that restored me to health as a child later on helped strengthen me when I became a mother myself, especially when I was blessed with a girl after three boys. I had a normal pregnancy, and there wasn't any reason to suspect trouble. But when my little girl, Marcie, was born, she was very yellow. The nurses didn't bring her to me when the other babies, who were also born that day, were brought in. Of course, I complained, not noticing the nurses exchanging worried glances. At last, to keep me quiet, they brought her to me, and when I saw her yellow skin, I understood their concern.

Most people are aware that if one parent has positive blood and the other parent has negative, complications usually result. Generally, in those cases, the doctors are alerted. What is less known is the problem when one blood type differs from another, such as one parent having type A blood and the other type O. This combination happens so rarely that doctors back then didn't always check for the possibility of the blood types "fighting" each other. This was what happened in my daughter's case.

I later found out that the nurses asked the doctor to talk to me before it was time to bring the babies to their mothers again. The doctor was the only pediatrician in Cheyenne, Wyoming, in 1962. My doctor explained that Marcie was in such critical shape that she would probably need four complete exchanges of blood. If the four exchanges of blood didn't work, she would either die or be severely retarded.

I remember the thought coming to me, *I must get the priesthood here to give her a blessing at once.* Warmth and comfort wrapped around me at that moment, and all doubt left my mind. I knew she would be healed. I often feel humbled, even today, at my complete confidence in my Heavenly Father that day.

But there was a problem. It was conference time in Salt Lake City, and most of the worthy priesthood leaders from our one small ward in Cheyenne had gone to Salt Lake. But remembering the faith of my mother, I did not give up. I knew that if I did all I could, the way would open. It took several frantic phone calls to locate two worthy priesthood brethren who could come to the hospital.

By the time they arrived, the doctors had given my daughter two exchanges of blood, but there had been no improvement in her condition. Then, because Marcie was in intensive care and it was a Catholic hospital, I had to get permission from the mother superior for the two men to give Marcie the blessing. Again, I turned to prayer. I prayed that I could explain to the mother superior how important this was so she would allow the men to bless my baby. Without this woman's permission, it would have been impossible.

The mother superior turned out to be a very sweet, understanding lady. Still, I'll never forget her saying, "It really isn't necessary for them to enter her room. We believe prayers pass through glass. Don't you?"

"Oh yes, yes, I do, but we believe in the laying on of hands. Please allow these representatives of my church to bless her in that way."

As I plead with her, tears overflowed my eyes. The mother superior looked at me for a long moment and then said, "I'll allow the men to scrub and go in to her."

I couldn't go in to be with them, but I soon heard the stories of what happened. It was all over the entire hospital that there was an extremely sick, yellow baby who had received two blood exchanges but hadn't improved. Then, miraculously, as the two Latter-day Saint elders finished their blessing, she started to turn pink even before they left the isolation unit.

One doctor in the hospital, a convert to the Church, later told my brother, who was his friend, how the nurses and other doctors were astounded at the miracle. I hoped some of them might one day agree to hear the gospel as a result.

My brother, H. Smith Shumway, a Church patriarch, was one of those attending conference in Salt Lake City. He had been blinded and severely wounded during World War II. When he returned from conference, I told him how desperately I'd wanted him to be the one to bless Marcie. He said something I'll always remember: "Any worthy man, regardless of his station in life or in the Church, has as much strength and power as any other." He also reminded me that my faith had played an important role in Marcie's healing.

Many small miracles, if there is such a thing as a "small" miracle, have happened in my life. I have learned how important it is to show gratitude for the blessings that are received and to acknowledge the bounty of blessings we can receive from our Heavenly Father, if we so desire. He stands waiting for us to ask.

Beth Shumway Moore is a snowbird who lives in Hurricane, Utah, during the winter but returns to Brigham City, Utah, during the summer. She has a master's degree from the University of Utah and taught school for thirty years. Now that her four children are grown, she enjoys grandchildren, church involvement, service with various charity groups, and her association with writers' groups in St. George, Utah.

A soft answer turneth away wrath: but grievous words stir up anger.

—Proverbs 15:1

I Snapped Back

by Sara Hacken

I teach in a large junior high school. After school started one fall, I received notice that all teachers were to turn in a report on a certain day. I worked on the report and had it ready, but I left school early to attend a training meeting on the day it was due, and I did not remember to drop it off until later. I decided to take it to the secretary first thing the next morning.

Early the next morning, I walked into the mail room to get my mail. Usually, it's very quiet, with few people around. I intended to go from there directly to my classroom, pick up the report, and put it in the secretary's box by the time she arrived.

However, as I reached for my mail, the secretary emerged from her office and lit into me before I could even get to my classroom. She let me know how inconsiderate I had been, how busy she was, and how much trouble I had caused by failing to give her the report on time.

I bristled, snapped back, and marched to my classroom to get the report, angry and upset that she hadn't even given me a chance to explain.

Later, however, I hated the feelings I had. I faced a year working with this woman and didn't want or need this kind of tension in the air all the time.

That night I took it to the Lord in prayer. How could I move forward this year with such angry words between us? The following day I still didn't have any idea of what to do. I got to the school and felt apprehensive. And, sure enough, right away we ran into each other in the mail room. Then, quietly, *in that very moment,* specific words came into my mind. I turned to her and smiled. "Boy, I hope today is a better day than yesterday. I don't know about you, but I was pretty stressed."

She replied, "I was having a horrible day. I feel bad about what I said."

It took only two minutes to heal the tension between us because of the help and direction I received from the Spirit. What might have made an entire year uncomfortable was over quickly. I am so grateful I took this small matter to the Lord in prayer and that He was gracious enough to know my heart and to allow me a way to mend the rift that had opened between us.

Sara Hacken, a teacher in Alpine School District, lives in Orem, Utah. She is a Gospel Doctrine teacher, a mother of five and grandmother to seven little boys, and loves literature, Church history, walking, and playing with her grandchildren.

And it shall be given them even according to the prayer of faith.

—D&C 93:52

My Diamond!

by Dorothy Varney

Early experiences in childhood can build faith for later challenges. As a child, I learned I could trust the Lord to help me; I would need that knowledge to support me through trials later on in my life.

One day when I was young, I opened the back door and entered the kitchen in tears. Mother heard my sobs, and we rushed into each other's arms.

"What is it? What is so terrible to upset my little girl?"

"It's Becky. She hates me."

"Oh, surely not. What makes you think that?"

"We were playing dolls and dressing them in the other's clothes. She said I tore her doll's best dress, but I didn't, Mother. Honest, I didn't. It was torn when she handed it to me."

"There, there," she said, stroking my hair.

"She's my best friend. Now she hates me. How could she think I did that?"

"You know what you need to do, don't you?"

I thought a few seconds, and then I knew.

"I have to pray, don't I?"

"You know what the Lord says: Pray about everything we do, the little things and the big things. It always makes you feel better, doesn't it?"

"Yes. But she really hurt my feelings. I almost hate her too."

"Well, then . . ."

I went to the kitchen chair and knelt down. Mother knelt beside me.

"Heavenly Father," I began, and then I choked with sobs. I dabbed at my eyes with Mother's handkerchief before going on. "My friend and I had a quarrel because she thinks I tore her doll's dress, but I didn't. Please help her to know I didn't. Or help her to forgive me and not hate me anymore."

As I closed my prayer, my crying stopped, and I stood up, just as I heard a knock at the kitchen door.

Mother answered it because my face was still stained with tears.

"Hello, Becky. Won't you come in?"

"I just wanted to tell Dorothy I'm sorry."

I couldn't believe it. Her face was tearstained, too. I walked to her, and we shared a hug.

"I was wrong, Dorothy," she said. "Mama says my doll's dress was already torn. I should have believed you."

"That's all right," I said. "I'm glad you don't hate me anymore."

"I could never hate you. I felt bad about what I said. And Mama says best friends should believe each other."

"My mother says Heavenly Father always helps us when things go wrong, if we ask and believe He will." I looked at Mother and saw a glow on her face. "She was right."

I learned about the power of prayer that day. It was one more incident in a small child's experience that helped to build a firm belief that God really listens to our prayers and will help us solve our problems if we believe He will. That belief carried over into my adult life and brought me to my knees to cry over the worries of raising my children, keeping love in my marriage, helping my husband through serious illnesses, magnifying my church callings, and what might seem to be trivial things, like losing the diamond from my wedding ring.

I had been shopping at the supermarket and came home with paper bags filled with produce, staple foods, and frozen goods. As I finished unloading and putting the groceries away, I glanced at my left hand and saw that the diamond was missing from the setting of my engagement ring. I gasped and frantically searched through the empty bags, the cupboards, the refrigerator, and the wastebaskets. No luck. I examined the ground between the house and the garage and scrutinized the area around the seats and floor of the car—to no avail.

I returned to the house and phoned the market, which seemed a ridiculous thing to do. How would one even begin to find a diamond among the produce displays or in the frozen-food bins or the shelves of cereal and cookies? I had been all over the store, and it would be like searching for a needle in a haystack. Nevertheless, I asked them to watch and let me know if someone found it. My heart sank as I left my name and phone number.

The diamond was my first and only—the one my husband had chosen to give me as he proposed, the one that thrilled me with its beauty and sparkle. It symbolized many years of life and love and hardships faced. It had become a part of me, of who I was. And now it was gone.

With the phone still in my hand, I asked myself, "What's wrong with me? I know what I have to do."

I hung up, went to the bedroom, and knelt by the bed.

"Heavenly Father, I know this is only the loss of a material thing that upsets me, but Thou hast counseled us to pray to Thee about everything in our households. This diamond is more than a material thing to me, as it has great sentimental value. It represents the love between me and my husband. I pray that Thou wilt guide me to know how I might find it, if that is possible. Inspire me to know where to look."

I rose from my knees and felt an urgency to search the car again. I went directly to the garage and opened the door on the driver's side. There, on the floor, between the door and seat, was the diamond! I had looked there thoroughly once before. But there it was, gleaming at me like a star. I hardly dared reach to pick it up, lest it prove not real. Yet, there it was, real and tangible.

Emotion welled within me, not just for the recovery of a diamond but also for assurance that in a world filled with monumental problems, my Heavenly Father cared and understood about my personal loss. It was one more proof that God hears and answers our prayers when we believe. The answer to my supplication as a small child laid the foundation for a lifetime of almost daily, similar experiences that today continue to sustain me as an elderly woman.

Dorothy Varney, from California, now resides with her daughter, Laurel Paul, in Washington, Utah. At eighty-six years young, she volunteers at an independent living center, actively participates in writers' groups, and attends meetings of the Daughters of the Utah Pioneers. She has held numerous Church positions, including serving a mission with her husband in the Fiji Islands. Mother of four children, she has eleven grandchildren and thirteen great-grandchildren.

My God hath been my support.

—2 Nephi 4:20

The Watch

by Donna Marley

Several years ago when I was a young mother, I was asked to teach a Relief Society lesson on faith. I agreed, but the thought of getting up in front of all those women with so much experience in the Church frightened me. Not only that, but I was asked to be sure to end ten minutes before the hour, leaving time for testimonies.

I didn't have any idea how to prepare a lesson that would fit so exactly into the given time frame. What if I went over? What if I didn't have enough material? Or worse, what if there wasn't a clock on the wall where I could see it? And if there was one, what if it wasn't working?

For some reason, this became a point of anxiety for me. If I could prepare enough material, I felt I'd be okay *as long as I could see a clock.*

On the morning of the lesson, I fished out my old watch, which I hadn't worn in five years. It didn't work. Of course it didn't work. It had been sitting unused for years. I could feel tears threaten. I *needed* this watch to work so I could have the confidence to give the lesson and stay within the proper time frame. I just really, really needed the watch to work!

I prayed, pleading for help. I was so nervous, and now I had this extra worry. I gave it a shake and then decided I would just set it to the right time anyway, which I did. And, suddenly, the hands were moving. The watch was working after all. Relief flooded me. Perhaps my prayers had been answered.

I taught the lesson, and everything went fine. I ended the lesson at ten minutes before our closing time—just right.

Soon after, vastly relieved, I got in the car and drove home with my family. I glanced at my watch, and it was 12:35 PM. I put it away.

Four years passed, and according to the regular rotation of Relief Society lessons, we were studying again from the same book. One day I was asked to substitute in Relief Society. When I opened the book, I found that I had been asked to teach *the very same lesson* I had taught four years earlier!

Out of curiosity, I went to get the old watch. Maybe it still worked. But no, it was stopped . . . at 12:35. How odd. That exact time triggered a memory. Wasn't that the time I had returned home after our meetings when I last gave this lesson? That meant the watch had stopped running the minute I took it off.

Suddenly, I understood. That day four years earlier, as I was about to give a lesson on faith, I had also been given a personal lesson on faith! The Lord had let the old watch run for the little over three hours it had been on my wrist, but that was all. The watch had run on faith—an answer to prayer for a very nervous teacher.

I have often thought back on that experience. I had just needed that one small help to feel confident enough to teach that day, and the Lord had kindly granted it. I was overcome as I contemplated what a loving gesture that was. I was given a lesson on faith that day that I didn't fully learn until four years later!

Donna Marley lives on Camano Island, just north of Seattle, Washington. She and her husband, Doug, enjoy spending time with their large family, camping, sailing, and participating in Church activities.

And they shall also teach
their children to pray, and to walk uprightly
before the Lord.

—D&C 68:28

Lost at the Flats

by Michael B. Thelin

Our family was on our way to spend a fun weekend at Chilao Flats, our favorite campground in the California mountains near our home. My mother, a young widow, had recently remarried, and as a result our family had suddenly grown larger, so I now had a stepbrother, Jim, who was older than me (I was eight at the time). And while we were all active members of the Church, Jim never seemed to care much about religion.

Jim and I spent a lot of time exploring the area, and I'd found a large stream some distance away. Jim wanted to explore the stream with me, so we set off over the hill to find it. It was a hot, dry day, not unusual for that time of year in the Sierra Nevadas. The cool stream would be a welcome change. We hiked over a final hill and found the river at the bottom of a steep ravine. Jim ran down the ravine ahead of me, trusting my ability to make my own way down, even though I was much smaller.

As we splashed in the water, Jim examined the steep ravine. "You know, a ravine this steep must have a waterfall in it, don't you think?"

"Maybe there's one downstream, around the bend," I said.

"Yeah, I dare you to find it!"

"That's easy. I'll be right back."

Confidently, I headed downstream. But soon I began to wonder if I was doing the right thing. My new stepbrother often seemed to push me farther than he did himself and then followed my lead. But because I was only eight, I didn't want to look like I was afraid, so I marched confidently downstream.

"Hey, Jim! I think I can hear a waterfall," I called back to him. "Maybe it's around the next bend."

"Hold up! I'm coming too," he called back as he splashed down the hill behind me. We came around a bend, but there was no waterfall.

"I think I can hear it," I said. So we kept going.

After several dozen "around the next bends," we gave up. There was no waterfall. And now it was very late in the day. So late, in fact, that we decided to take a shortcut across the hill, eliminating several of the bends in the river. We headed out through the woods and climbed over the hill, but we didn't recognize anything. We decided to keep going, assuming the campground was probably just over the next rise. We hiked up that rise and then another, but there was no sign of the campground . . . or the stream. In the gathering dusk, every direction seemed to look the same. Which way to go?

Jim was getting worried. "Mike, I think we're lost. I don't even know the way back to the stream."

"What should we do?"

"I don't know. Let's climb up to the top of the next hill and see if we can find the stream."

"I was taught that if you're lost you should stay where you are."

"Yeah, I know," said Jim. "But Mom will be mad at me if I don't get us home."

That was probably true. He was older, and Mom knew he liked to egg me on. Then my new stepbrother surprised me.

"Mike, I'm scared," he admitted. His voice took on an unusual intensity. "I don't know much about God or church or anything, but I know you do. Would you please say a prayer for us?"

I had been praying for as long as I could remember. I had always been taught that we had a Heavenly Father who cared about us. Yet his request surprised me. He had told me a lot of times that he didn't believe in God. But maybe he really did. I just wished that I had thought of it first. "Okay. No problem," I replied at last.

We knelt in the dirt and folded our arms.

"Dear Heavenly Father, we seem to be lost. Would you please help us find our way back to the family? Thanks for this wonderful forest and all that you have given us."

When I closed the prayer, Jim heaved a deep sigh, and I knew he had liked that we prayed. "What do we do now?" he asked expectantly.

Even though I had been taught to pray, I suddenly wondered what the next step was. Was I supposed to hear a voice or something? Unsure, my eye fell on a small game trail. "How about we follow that small trail over there, and we can decide what to do next."

We started walking along a small deer trail that wound off around the hillside.

"Should we climb to the top of the hill so we can see something?" Jim asked.

I didn't want to do that. I felt a trail had to go someplace, and I didn't want to lose sight of it. "No. I feel better just following this trail. Let's continue for a little while."

"I suppose."

After a few minutes of walking, we came upon some Indian potholes.

"Mike, look!" Jim exclaimed. "Aren't these the potholes near our camp?"

"They sure are! I know where we are!" Excited, I took off. "Follow me!"

Moments later I found the main trail. As we ran toward camp, we could hear Mom calling us. The sound of her voice was the most wonderful sound in the world at that moment. We knew we were safe.

I was only eight years old that day, but I've never forgotten that it wasn't until I knelt in prayer that the ideas came to me that took us to safety. I've applied that same lesson many times in the years since, always with the same hope that one day I will be led safely home.

Michael Thelin, father of six and grandfather of five, lives in Pleasant Grove, Utah. He enjoys wood carving, playing with his grandchildren, and spending time in the mountains with his family.

*And they were all young men, and
they were exceedingly valiant for courage, and
also for strength and activity; but behold, this was not all—
they were men who were true at all times in
whatsoever thing they were entrusted.*

—Alma 53:20

What Should He Do?

Name Withheld

It is a difficult time to be a teenager. It is easy to accept some awful behavior as normal because we see it all the time. But it can still come as a surprise when it hits close to home.

My son was playing video games in his friend's bedroom when his friend asked him if he would like to do some things of an immoral nature. Shocked, my son said no and left immediately. Over the next couple of weeks, this friend would pressure my son at Scouts, at church, and at other activities. It seemed that once the possibility had been introduced between them, his friend felt more confident in bringing it up and trying to get my son involved.

My son didn't know what to do and took it to the Lord in prayer, asking for help and to know what the right thing to do was. The next Sunday, he had a feeling he should talk to the bishop after church. This took a lot of courage, and I don't think he would have been brave enough to talk about his longtime friend without having gone to the Lord in prayer first and then receiving such a strong impression. He knew he was being led to get help.

He went in and told the bishop what happened with his friend, who was also a member of the ward. The bishop thanked him and told him he had done the right thing in coming in to talk with him. The bishop quietly called in the other boy's parents and explained what had happened. They were shocked, and the family went into counseling.

It has been over a year now, and today they are a stronger, healthier family. If my son had kept quiet, nothing could have been healed, and who can say what kind of problems his friend would be dealing with today?

Keeping quiet or avoiding the young man wasn't the right solution. Taking the problem to the Lord and having the courage to act on the inspiration given was courageous and the right thing to do.

My son has seen for himself that the Lord will help steer him through unexpected problems. Thank goodness for prayer. Thank goodness for the Church for setting sensible guidelines and standards. And thank goodness for teenagers who take their problems to the Lord and then listen to promptings.

But if ye will . . . put
your trust in him, and serve him with
all diligence of mind . . . he will, according to his
own will and pleasure, deliver you.

—Mosiah 7:33

We Held On In Faith

by Janice Stringham LeFevre

After running errands with my kids, I pulled into the garage and noticed that my husband, Steve, was home an hour earlier than normal. That was very unusual. I felt a vague uneasiness as I considered why he might have left work early. The kids and I got out of the car and headed inside. Steve was at the door, and he greeted me with an ashen face and no trace of his usual smile.

A small quiver of alarm rippled through me. Silent signals passed between us, and I knew I needed to talk to him alone. We headed into our bedroom. He sunk into a chair and looked down, dejected. His journal lay open on the bed, and I could see he'd been writing before I arrived home. I slid the journal over and sat on the bed, facing Steve. I reached for his hand; it shook slightly, and I could see he was working hard to hold back tears. My alarm increased.

"What happened?" I asked, attempting to keep the tension out of my voice.

Steve hesitated, and he looked at me. "Our entire engineering team is being laid off. I've got just thirty days to find a new job."

The shock hung, pulsing in the air until it penetrated my skin and settled deep into my stomach and soured. I felt nauseated. After months of uncertainty, it had happened. Steve had known that layoffs were a possibility. We'd even discussed whether he should begin looking for another job, since finding a new position in the post–September 11 economic downturn would not be easy. We'd prayed about it for months, and the impressions that came to each of us were to stay where we were because the Lord had a great blessing in store for us. We'd believed this meant that Steve's job as a government contractor would be safe.

Now I feared we'd misinterpreted the Spirit's guidance. Had we imposed our own desires onto those spiritual impressions and inadvertently twisted their meaning? My mind raced with the implications of making such a serious blunder. Since our twelve-year-old son was a cancer survivor and still under medical supervision, we had to have health insurance. Did we have enough savings? If not, how would we pay the medical bills and mortgage? I felt my world tilting into the unknown.

I reached out, and in a moment Steve's arms were around me. We both needed the comfort and security we felt in one another's arms. *Thank goodness we have each other. No matter what happens, at least we'll always have that.*

After a few quiet minutes, Steve said, "The job market is tight. I don't know how I can possibly find something quickly enough. Right now, the average time for engineers to land a job is four to six months, sometimes longer." He paused. "We can't last that long."

"There's got to be something out there that's available now," I said, trying to push my doubts aside.

Steve reached for his journal. "I started brainstorming ideas before you got home. I've made a list of guys I know at other companies. I can call them tomorrow, but I'm not too hopeful. Some of these places may be laying off, too." He showed me the list. It seemed pathetically short—only three local and two out-of-state possibilities.

"We can also get your résumé out on the Internet." *But,* I thought, *there's probably hundreds of electrical engineers already registered who've been unemployed for months.*

We discussed our savings and other emergency resources. We figured that by reducing our expenses to a necessities-only budget, we could pay our mortgage and bills for about three months without additional income.

"Thank goodness we have our food storage," I said, "or it could be a lot worse. Plus, we've always paid our tithing and fast offerings, so we can count on the Lord to help us." I knew this to be true, but I also knew that God's timetable can be so different from ours, and His purposes are generally not very clear to us in the midst of trials. This was going to call for a great deal of faith. As much as I wanted the answers now—as much as I wanted to know we wouldn't lose everything—I still needed to put it in His hands.

Steve spoke up. "As I drove home today, I had a strong feeling come to me that the way we handle this situation is important because we must show our faith and be good examples to the kids."

I nodded. "We need to be sure they see how we rely on the Lord to get us through this trial. It can build their faith."

He gave me a half grin. "This isn't exactly the way I intended to teach our children more about having faith, but I guess it works." He shrugged.

"The good thing is that we *do* trust that the Lord will see us through."

We finally emerged from the bedroom and sat down with the children. We told them that their dad had lost his job and that this would entail some changes in our lifestyle. We reassured them that even though we didn't yet know where he would be working next, we did know Heavenly Father was watching over us.

That night my brother gave my husband a priesthood blessing, in which he told Steve that the Lord was preparing a way for him to provide for our family. He was counseled to draw upon our memories of times when barriers had appeared impossible to surmount and how the Lord had helped us to conquer them. We were then to use those memories as springboards to bolster our faith.

As my brother articulated the Lord's counsel, I received a spiritual confirmation that the words being spoken were true. Knowing that I could rely on the Lord's promise that Steve would find a job, I was comforted and felt a measure of peace.

However, I was still anxious about the details. How long would he be unemployed? Would we have to go a period of time without medical insurance? Would we have to move? Nevertheless, I now felt I could move forward with confidence that God was with us and would sustain us, come what may.

Yet, it was sometimes a challenge to move ahead, day after day, in faith. No news today. Nothing yet. How long until something happened? Several nights I allowed doubts to creep in until I was too stressed to sleep. Sometimes anxiety made my stomach feel like I'd just eaten a lump of salt dough laced with Tabasco sauce.

However, each day I focused intently on choosing to have faith in the Lord's promises that Steve would find work. This helped me to overcome the deep fear that was waiting to drag me down. I often prayed for another spiritual confirmation that we would be fine, and I consciously and deliberately left my worries in the Lord's hands.

Finding and retaining peace proved to be harder for Steve. His job loss was more difficult for him to face because it directly attacked one of his central, God-ordained roles as husband and father—that of providing the necessities of life for his family. He felt like he'd failed us, and that made him depressed, miserable, and shaken. It was very difficult for me to see him this way. He was usually the ballast keeping me at an even keel; now I needed to be that for him.

During that time, we began to take steps to do all in our power to solve the problem. Steve and I updated his résumé. He called his engineering friends and scoured the Internet for job leads. At home, I searched the want ads and prayed intensely for guidance, not only to help him find employment, but also to know how to buoy him up under his crushing burden of responsibility. I reread the notes I'd taken during Steve's blessing and got an idea. I decided that even though it was Friday, we could have a family home evening that night. It could be a means to not only comfort Steve, but also to teach the children. I prayerfully prepared a lesson.

When Steve got home late that afternoon, he looked like his spirit had been pummeled by a truckload of heavy bricks. He was completely discouraged. I told him about my idea to hold a family home evening, and he readily agreed.

After dinner, we gathered the children. Steve and I spoke frankly about the implications of our possible long-term unemployment and the family budget cuts we were making. Everyone looked glum.

"Things are not as bad as they seem, though," I said. "Do you remember in Dad's blessing that he was promised that he would be able to find a job?"

They nodded. Steve tried to look positive; at best, he looked stoic.

"I know we can trust in the Lord's promises, but all of us have to do our part, too. Looking for a new job is not enough. We also need to show our faith. We do this by fasting and praying— telling Heavenly Father that we believe His promises, asking for His guidance, and then following it. We demonstrate faith by being obedient to His commandments and making personal sacrifices. This shows the Lord that we are willing to do all in our power to receive this blessing. It's important that we also remember that even when we do everything we can to obtain the blessings we desire, sometimes the Lord lets us struggle for a while—sometimes a long while, even a lifetime—because He knows what is best for us. Sometimes we have lessons to learn that can only come through that struggle."

As a family, we read scripture verses, such as Mormon 9:19–21 and Doctrine and Covenants 82:10 and 130:20–21, where the Lord promises to bless us if we have sufficient faith in Christ and if we are willing to obey the law upon which the blessing is predicated.

I then recounted two family stories when we'd faced severe problems and overwhelming roadblocks. I highlighted the patterns of faith, obedience, and sacrifice that we'd followed, which had sustained and comforted us and helped us exercise the faith needed so we could draw upon heaven's powers to assist us. In each situation, the Lord had blessed us with miraculous interventions.

I repeatedly peeked at Steve from the corner of my eye, hoping these memories would help him to feel better—more confident, less afraid. As I spoke, I also felt the Spirit swell within me until I was saturated with refreshment and warmth.

By the end of the lesson, I recognized that my family was feeling the Spirit's manifestations, as well—the children's eyes shone, and Steve had slowly relaxed and settled into his chair. He looked at me and gave me a gentle smile.

"Thank you," he said. "I think we all needed that reminder. I know I did." He turned to the kids. "I feel the Spirit here with us tonight. Can you feel it, too?"

They smiled and nodded.

"That's the Lord's witness that what your mom said is true. Sometimes it's easy to be scared, and it's hard to have faith when things are not the way we want them. I've felt that way today. So it's good to remember times when the Lord has helped us. It helps us feel calm again."

"Remembering these stories can also give us confidence that since the Lord has helped us in the past, He will help us now," I said. "Let's think of what we can do to show our faith."

We then discussed ideas about what we could sacrifice and how we could be more obedient to the commandments. We also decided to have a family fast the next Sunday.

In the coming weeks, our situation often looked pretty bleak. For instance, one day Steve came home with disconcerting news about the only openings he'd found in our local area. There were enough positions available at a nearby government facility to hire him as well as the rest of his engineering group. However, politically motivated opposition had successfully obstructed their employment.

"It looks like we'll have to move out of state," Steve voiced with a sigh, as we discussed our options one evening while lying in bed. "I'll follow up on that job possibility in Baltimore. They called me today. They're very interested."

The news should have made me happy, but this was the one solution I'd dreaded most. I did not want to move—especially clear across the country, with our son still under medical supervision. After living in multiple places, I was also grateful to finally have a permanent home and a wonderful community in which to raise our children.

Tears flooded my eyes. I tried to blink them away so Steve wouldn't see. It was no use.

He looked over at me in the lamplight and saw my tears. "What's wrong?" he asked. He drew me closer to his side; I snuggled up to him and laid my head on his shoulder.

"I'm sorry. I don't mean to cry," I said as more tears began to flow, putting dark, wet splotches on his blue pajamas. "I don't want to seem ungrateful. It's just hard to think about leaving here and moving so far from our parents and friends."

"I wish we had a closer option," he said, "but right now this seems the only one."

I knew he was right and that he needed my support. After a long moment, I softly whispered, "I want you to know that I am willing to move if that's where the Lord wants us."

Together, we prayed to see if the Lord wanted Steve to take the job in Baltimore. We felt the Spirit bring us peace, but we did not feel a confirmation. I thought it was because Steve did not yet have an official job offer. So Steve continued the job hunt, but there was nothing more available. We continued to seek a confirmation, but it did not come. What did it all mean?

Some days the uncertainty was excruciating. Steve and I prayed for strength and wisdom and continued to apply gospel principles so we could hold on in faith. Another week went by. Then one of Steve's former coworkers called to tell him of a job opening. A government engineer was unexpectedly promoted out of a crucial job, and they needed a replacement fast. They wanted someone with very specialized qualifications and expertise. When they'd learned that Steve was looking for a job, they were thrilled; he had the exact skills they needed. As soon as we heard about this job, the Spirit witnessed that this was the right place for Steve to work. Suddenly, we had solid evidence to confirm our hope and confidence in the Lord's promises.

After more prayers and several small miracles involving the cutting of red tape and the softening of two hearts, Steve was hired. We experienced a significant pay cut and had to make some lifestyle changes, but we did not have to move.

Amazingly, Steve's new job began the day after his lay-off went into effect; we didn't go even one day without medical benefits. His new working conditions were better than he'd ever experienced before in his career. He loved his new work assignments. He was valued and respected. Plus, he now had more time to spend with us.

As we look back at these events, Steve and I still marvel at the Lord's hand in our lives. Heavenly Father knew that Steve didn't need to look for employment before he was laid off because He'd prepared the way so that when he needed a new job, the ideal one would become available. This experience increased our confidence in interpreting and following spiritual promptings. It also gave us an opportunity to let our children see that faith is not always an easy choice—that doubts and fears strive hard to torpedo it—but when we choose faith, we can be at peace even during our trials. And sometimes the Lord will even work miracles in our behalf.

Janice Stringham LeFevre is a mother of three, historian, freelance writer, and poet. Janice enjoys historical research, reading, traveling, playing games, and boogie boarding in the Pacific Ocean. She has served in various Church callings, including a full-time mission. Married to Steven Ronald LeFevre, she lives in Kaysville, Utah.

*For we labor diligently to
write, to persuade our children, and also
our brethren, to believe in Christ, and to be reconciled
to God; for we know that it is by grace that we
are saved, after all we can do.*

—*2 Nephi 25:23*

Dead-end Road

by Judy C. Olsen

One summer I was spending a few days vacationing high in the deeply forested camp area on Cedar Mountain, outside Cedar City, Utah, with my three daughters, ages ten, seven, and four. My husband and son were home working—three hours away in Nevada.

One afternoon my daughters and I piled into our large van and took off exploring. We found a newly graded road that took off through the heavily wooded area. It meandered through the trees, and we became very curious to see where it led. Pines and lofty maples hugged us close on both sides, and the canopy of branches above shaded us from direct sunlight.

After traveling for what seemed like a long time, we came around a bend and . . . the road suddenly ended in the middle of the forest. Large piles of dirt marked where a grader had simply stopped plowing the new road. There was nothing but heavily timbered woods in every direction. I braked, feeling a little disappointed, but it was such a nice day that we could just go back and find someplace else to explore.

I expertly swung the van hard to the left, intending to turn around, but instead we sunk deep into loose dirt. I put the motor into reverse and stepped on the gas. The tires spun but did not move in the soft dirt. Apprehension gripped me. I tried again and then got out to see what I could do.

My front wheels were sunk up to the axles. The back wheels were not in as far; nevertheless, they only spun in the dirt. I got back into the driver's seat and tried putting the van into drive, then rocking back into reverse, then back into drive, again and again. We didn't move. If anything, we were now sunk deeper.

We were several miles from the forest-service connecting road, and I could hear cars passing distantly along the highway, but the sun was low in the sky. I considered my options. I could take the girls and hike back some miles the way we had come, leave the girls and hike back myself, or cut across through the woods to the highway and flag down a car. I decided my third option was the best idea. The back roads would soon be empty of cars, but the highway would always have someone coming along it, even after dark.

I set off through the woods, walking toward the distant sounds of automobiles. I crossed a shallow ravine and climbed to the top of the ridge beyond. Then I turned to look back at the van, sitting forlornly alone with my three daughters inside. I looked toward the sounds of cars, thinking they were very close and that I should have seen the road through the trees by now. But all I saw was another ravine and another ridge. Once I left the ridge top where I stood, I'd no longer be able to see where I had come from or where I was going. In every direction the trees looked the same. I paused. I could so easily become disoriented in the lengthening shadows of the endless woods.

Maybe the highway was close—and maybe not. Maybe the sounds just carried in the late afternoon air. I couldn't leave the girls alone in the car in the middle of nowhere. I turned back, unsure what to do.

When I got back, I carefully looked at the van. The only thing I could think of was to push some leaves, twigs, and pine branches behind the back tire. Maybe that would allow the van's wheels to get purchase on the soft dirt. With my daughters helping, we piled twigs and branches behind one of the back wheels, and then we all got in the car. I started the engine and slammed it into reverse. Nothing happened.

Discouraged, I got out. I began to pray to know what to do. The sun was getting lower in the sky. We had no food, no light, no blankets, and no water. We were woefully unprepared to spend a night in the woods. Our little afternoon drive had turned into a nightmare.

The idea occurred to me to use the car's jack to lift up one of the wheels. Gina, age ten, went to work pumping the handle up and down, raising the rear tire by inches. The rest of us gathered twigs and leaves and a few dead branches and stuffed them in the hole under the wheel.

Feeling hopeful, we piled into the car and started the engine. I put the car into reverse . . . and we didn't move. I stopped again and got out to look. All the twigs and branches had been thrown out from under the wheel.

Over the next hour, we tried again and again to jack up the back tire and load the space under it with increasingly larger branches. Then we decided to jack up both back tires, one after the other, and place twigs and branches under them—but to no avail.

It was nearly dark now. Apprehension was turning to fear. No one knew where we were. I had to try again. I didn't know what else to do. This just had to work! First, we raised one back tire. Then the other back tire. Then one of the front tires. I got in thinking that surely this time we'd get out.

I bowed my head and offered a prayer. I explained that I was tired, my children young, and we had no food or water. The night would soon get very cold. Would the Lord please help us?

Into my mind came the words, *Have you done all you can do?*

Shocked, I thought of the last front tire still sitting on the dirt. I reasoned with the Spirit. *I'm just a woman with three little girls, and I've tried for hours to move this van. Won't Thou please bless us?* I just felt I couldn't do one more tire and that the Lord might look with compassion upon my difficulty. Hoping against hope, I started the car, put it into reverse . . . and nothing happened.

But . . . had I been given a key?

We began again with the back tires, jacking up one, then the second, stuffing twigs and branches under each one. Then we started on the front tires, this time doing both of them. I was done. I had no more ideas, no more strength, no more daylight. I had done all in my power.

I turned to the kids. "Okay, kids. We all need to fold our arms and pray. We've done everything we know to do, and we need help."

My three girls knelt together in the backseat and prayed silently. I bowed my head in prayer with a pure heart and asked for the Lord to help us, explaining that I had done everything in my power that I knew to do. I was at the limit of my earthly knowledge and understanding of how to solve this problem. I was close to the physical limit of what I could do. I closed my prayer quietly and took a deep breath. This was it.

I put the car into gear and stepped on the gas pedal. The tires began to spin. Suddenly, the car *leaped up and out of the soft dirt* as though a giant hand had pushed us. We went flying across the road, nearly landing in the soft dirt on the opposite side.

The girls started shouting in joy, and I heard Gina say, "Mom! I just prayed that the Lord would send an angel to push us out! And He did!"

I agreed. That was *exactly* how it felt. I turned back the way we had come and carefully drove the darkened and empty road before us, gratitude washing over me. It was reverent in our car on that trip home. We all knew, in a way we'd never forget, that after all we can do, the Lord is there to help us.

Judy C. Olsen is a writer and editor. Her award-winning novel Beyond the Horizon, *was published in 2007. She is a former editor for the* Ensign *magazine. She and her husband, Don, have four children and fifteen grandchildren and reside in Sandy, Utah.*

Sweet Whisperings

Whoso putteth his trust in the LORD *shall be safe.*

—Proverbs 29:25

A Day to Remember

by Shirley Manning

It was as normal as any summer day could be for me and my two daughters. After we sent my husband off to work and cleaned up the breakfast dishes that morning, I told my four-year-old daughter, Elizabeth, that she had been invited to play at the neighbor's house with her friend, William.

"Mommy, William is a big boy—he's five!" Elizabeth told me as she ran out our back door to the back door William's mom held open for her. I would retrieve her in one hour if everything went well.

Within just ten minutes, as I finished changing baby Katherine, a vivid picture suddenly came into my mind—the retention pond a block from our house that was filled with spring runoff water. In that moment I "saw" William running toward the water and Elizabeth squeezing under the eight-foot chain-link fence after him. So vivid and forceful was this image that it displaced all other conscious thoughts. Emotion shook me, almost like a burning under my skin.

With an urgency similar to a person under water needing to take a breath, I picked up Katherine and ran past the phone, out the door, and down the sidewalk as fast as I could with a two-year-old child in my arms. As I rounded the corner at the end of the block, I saw the same scene before me as I had seen in my mind. William had scooted under the fence and was scrambling toward the water, and Elizabeth had squeezed herself through the gap, except for one little heel.

"William, STOP!" I screamed with a voice I didn't know I had. Startled, he froze in place and so did Elizabeth. I hurried to the kid-size breach in the fence and pulled both children through. Tears of guilt made clean little tracks down their dirty cheeks.

"Mommy," Elizabeth sobbed, "how did you know we were here?"

I pulled the little ones close and whispered, "I knew it from Heavenly Father."

"Oh," Elizabeth said. Then she added, "We're in trouble, aren't we?"

"Yes. Yes, you are," I confirmed.

I picked up Katherine and started back up the sidewalk. Elizabeth and William followed. We walked home very slowly and silently. When I got to William's home, I explained to his mother what had happened. She paled at the news and admitted she had not realized that the two of them had slipped outside.

Later that night, I talked with my daughter about how much Heavenly Father loved both her and William. Because He knew they were in danger—even though *they* were unaware of it—He had sent help.

We knelt down, folded our arms, bowed our heads, and thanked Heavenly Father for putting such a vivid image in my mind that let me know Elizabeth and William were in danger.

"This was one way Heavenly Father answers prayers we ask every day," I explained, "like 'Please watch over us and keep us safe from harm' or 'Bless us to have Thy Spirit to be with us.'"

On that ordinary day, we had had an extraordinary experience that neither of us would ever forget. I know now that Heavenly Father sometimes helps mothers protect and even save their precious children from harm or death.

Later that night, sleepless, I was overcome with gratitude for the incredible blessing of the day. I thought of my innocent daughter and of her little friend and his thankful parents. Although Heavenly Father does not always save children from harm as he did my daughter that day, I know He loves all of His children and cares what happens to them. I was left grateful and humbled that this time she had been spared.

Shirley Manning and her husband, Marty, live in Kaysville, Utah. They have six children—five daughters and a son who is currently serving a mission—and eleven grandchildren. Shirley enjoys writing and gardening. She and her husband do many things together, including teaching Primary, playing golf and tennis, and going horseback riding.

Learn of me, and listen to my words;
walk in the meekness of my Spirit, and you
shall have peace in me.

—D&C 19:23

Call Home

by Donna Jean

One summer I had my heart set on going to girls camp with the Young Women. But about that time, we were able to adopt a child to add to our other nine. I told my husband that I wouldn't go this time so I could stay home with our new child.

Much to my surprise, he encouraged me to get away for a few days with the girls, as he knew how much it meant to me.

"Are you sure? The baby is only three months old."

"I'll be fine. Go ahead," he said.

So I left, along with two of my daughters, for girls camp.

We had a wonderful time. The camp was located in the mountains, far away from civilization. My cell phone didn't work, as I quickly found out when I tried calling home to see how things were going. But since I couldn't get through, I turned my attention to the girls and their activities.

One morning I had a strong impression that I should call home. It was so strong that I grabbed my cell phone and began walking the perimeter of the camp, hoping to find a cell service signal. After walking around the entire campsite, I knew there wasn't any place where I could pick up a cell signal.

But the feeling persisted, so I went into the woods to pray. I explained that I felt I needed to call home but that I couldn't get through. Then I had a feeling to try again, so I dialed, and, suddenly, the phone was ringing, and my husband answered!

He was relieved to hear my voice. One of the children had fallen and split open his lip. He couldn't find the first-aid supplies. We lived on a peninsula thirty minutes away from any stores, and there wasn't anywhere nearby to buy bandages. On top of that, there was so much confusion at home that he didn't know how to cope any longer. I told him where to look for the first-aid supplies, and as he patched up the split lip, we discussed other things going on at home. Soon his voice was calm again. He was going to be okay, he assured me.

I hung up twenty minutes later, grateful that we had been able to talk.

The next day I returned to the same spot to try to get a cell signal, thinking I would love to say hi again and see if all was well. But there was no signal. My phone was dead.

Again I prayed, but the phone didn't work. Then, into my mind came a gentle thought: *Yesterday there had been a need, but today the need isn't as great. But if I ever have a need, I have only to ask.*

I pondered on that, realizing that my prayers had been answered with special spiritual help the day before—and that if I ever really, really needed help, they would be answered again. The Lord does listen and answer prayers in some most unexpected ways when the need is important.

I am grateful to live in a day when we are privileged to receive many spiritual blessings that can help us with our everyday lives.

Donna Jean enjoys sewing, including making wedding dresses for her daughters and daughter-in-law. She and her husband are active in the Church and enjoy many activities with their children.

*The gifts of the Gospel are given to strengthen
the faith of the believer.*

*—Brigham Young, Discourses of Brigham Young,
selected and arranged by John A. Widtsoe, 1943, 161*

The Almost Vacation

by Liz Bennett

Some dates burn themselves clearly into your mind. For me, one of those memorable moments in my life came on December 26, 1987. I was twelve years old. My mother, two of my older brothers, and I had left the house early to drive the many miles from Phoenix, Arizona, to Logan, Utah, to visit my oldest brother and his family.

As usual, we got a late start. Nevertheless, Mother suddenly pulled over so we could have a family prayer, which we always did before traveling. We all dutifully closed our eyes while Mother asked for the standard things: safe travel and that the car wouldn't break down. Then we were on our way, and I settled in for a long drive—one I wasn't looking forward to because I had to share the backseat of our little Toyota Tercel with my fourteen-year-old brother, who I thought was a real pain to be around in those days.

About midmorning we approached the little town of Camp Verde in northern Arizona. Snow lined the highway, and we had the heater on. My brother thankfully had fallen asleep next to me, which gave me some peace, at least for a little while. My mother drove, and my other brother David sat in the passenger seat in front of me. I leaned my head on the window and watched the scenery go by, not really thinking about anything. Then a thought formed very clearly in my mind. *Does everyone have their seat belt on?* I sat up straight and spoke the question aloud—I couldn't help myself. Both occupants of the front seat checked their buckles.

I looked over at my sleeping brother, who was especially moody that day, even for a teenager. I hesitated. I knew he would not take kindly to his little sister waking him up just to make him put on his seat belt. Even the thought made me shudder.

I'm being silly, I told myself. *Why does it even matter?* I shook off the weird feeling and let him sleep. Nor did I bother to dig out my own seat belt from under the pillow I was sitting on to make my journey more comfortable. So both of us in the backseat remained unbelted.

Not five minutes after that thought came, we rounded a curve in the road, and the car hit a patch of black ice. The last thing I remember seeing was the side of the mountain in front of the car as we spun out of control, flipped upside down, and crumpled on the side of the road.

When I came to, I found myself lying in a heap against the roof of the car and the window. I called out to see if everyone was okay. My mother and brother in the front seat, secured in their seat belts, were all right. But my brother who had been asleep next to me was gone. I screamed.

My mom's leg was cut badly, and her foot had been pinned so she stayed in the car while David opened his door—the only one intact—and he and I crawled out and looked around. Passersby stopped to offer aid, some bringing blankets. I finally spotted my brother who had been sleeping next to me moments before. He appeared dazed as he walked around in the snow, bleeding but alive. He had a gash on his jawline and another on his leg. To this day I have no logical explanation of how he survived, as the place where he had been sitting had caved in completely in the crash.

As the details of the accident came together, it became apparent that my brother had been ejected from the car as it rolled, barely escaping getting crushed by the car as it flipped over. The front passenger side of the car had the only intact tire and door—even the window had escaped damage. The rest of the car looked like a spent sardine can. It's still incredible to me to think that four people had been inside, along with luggage and Christmas gifts, yet had escaped serious injury or death.

An ambulance arrived, and we were taken to the hospital in Camp Verde, where my mom and brother had their wounds stitched up. I had been banged around quite a bit and would be sore for weeks to come, but the two of us in the backseat had escaped serious damage. Neither one of us had even broken a bone. I'd left a hunk of my hair on the clothing hook near the back window but otherwise had no mark on me. My uncle drove up to bring us home that afternoon, so we spent the night safe in our beds.

This potential tragedy passed into our family's history as a significant event—but thankfully not as a day marked by the loss of loved ones. I have no explanation for why we all survived, except that perhaps Heavenly Father had further work for us upon the earth. I have thought much since that day about the impression I had received, and I have come to believe that it was a teaching moment from the Lord. That knowledge has since helped me recognize promptings at other times, only now I try to respond more fully.

In all His wisdom, the Lord understood that at age twelve I could not fully comprehend what to do with such an impression as I experienced. He, nevertheless, opened a way for my brother to be saved from serious harm. And who knows? Maybe it was better for him not to have been buckled in. We'll never really know. I do know that I probably would have fared better had I dug out my own seat belt and put it on. But lessons come as we are able to learn, and at the age of twelve, I had been given my first lesson in listening to the Spirit. Now I know how important it is to respond to promptings and to follow them. I know my family survived the accident by divine design.

Liz Bennett enjoys traveling and spending time with her family, especially at the same time. Some of her hobbies include reading the classics and writing, of course. Liz is active in her Church callings and is always up for a good laugh.

And I was led by the Spirit,
not knowing beforehand the things
which I should do.

—1 Nephi 4:6

Go Now!

by Carolyn Vawdrey

They say trials help make us stronger—help us grow. Usually our trials take us unawares—they are neither planned nor expected. And sometimes they seem just too hard to bear.

When I was in Young Women at the age of fifteen, a couple moved into our ward with a handicapped child. They taught us about her disability, how hard it was for their daughter to live her life in a wheelchair with nurses around the clock, and how her life expectancy would be short because of the disability.

A strong impression came over me that I, too, would have to face dealing with a child with a disability—maybe even one confined to a wheelchair or without limbs. In my heart I felt I could handle that.

After I married, our first son was born in the month of July, with ten fingers, ten toes, and all the major parts intact. I sighed with relief, knowing he would not be the child with the disability. Or so I thought.

Once he came home from the hospital, he stopped nursing. We called a nursing specialist to help, but even she was unable to get the baby to suck. I bought plastic nipples for his bottle and poked extra holes in them to get him to take the milk without difficulty. I did whatever I could to help him take nourishment.

Throughout his infancy he missed one major milestone after another: rolling over, sitting up, and crawling. I tried not to notice, telling myself he was a late bloomer and his time would come. He looked normal in all other respects. He would catch up.

It was not until he turned three that I finally acknowledged there was a problem. He had not begun to talk, not like most children. Oh, sure, he could list the planets of the solar system in order and sing his favorite theme song from *Bill Nye the Science Guy,* but he did not say any other words. When we would talk to him, he never looked us in the eyes. Again, I thought it would pass. It *had* to pass. I could not see anything physically wrong with him.

My mother-in-law suggested I take him to a special school for the disabled, where they helped children with speech problems. We made an appointment to see a speech therapist and did all the preliminaries—had his sight and hearing checked. It was not until I told her that he would only eat orange foods that she stopped what she was doing and got the psychologist. She said it might be something called autism, or Asperger's syndrome. I smiled and laughed at her in disbelief, hoping she was wrong.

Not long after that, my pediatrician confirmed our fears and asked us to see a specialist at the local university.

I drove home from my pediatrician's office. I knew they were wrong—they were all wrong. Tears flooded my sight and a pit formed in my stomach. *Why was this happening? What had I done wrong? Did I drop my child as an infant? Did I feed him the wrong foods?*

That night, unable to sleep, I knelt down and asked Heavenly Father to help me, to let me know what I needed to do. A memory came back to me—the couple with the handicapped daughter. I recalled the feelings I had had at the time, that I would be able to handle it. I realized my challenge didn't involve a wheelchair or missing limbs—my child had all his body parts intact; there was something else affecting him.

As I prayed, I felt a strong spirit of assurance that the child born to our home was special, not just because of his disabilities but also because he had a special mission in life. There was a reason he came to me, to our family. Not only would blessings fill his life, but blessings would come to our family, too. This understanding profoundly comforted me. It was the first night in months that I had gone to bed in peace. I would continue to search for answers to help my child, and things would eventually be okay, even if they did not seem so now.

Fall had come. One day as I did my dishes, I watched the red leaves outside my window blow in the wind. A sudden urge to call the university flooded over me. Although I did not know why, I felt strongly guided to do so. Without hesitation, I simply picked up the phone book and searched for the name of the treatment center the pediatrician had given me. As I dialed the number with shaky fingers, my mind raced, contemplating possible reasons for such urgency.

A man answered the phone and explained to me that there was a chance for me to get my son into a special program for autistic children if his symptoms matched certain criteria. I would need to come in to see if he fit the requirements. I hung up the phone, wondering if I had done the right thing. Would this guide me to an answer for my child's problems?

My heart sped up as I again felt a prompting, this time to do it *now*. I grabbed my child and rushed to the center. There I found out my son's requirements were off by only small margins, but the signs that I had described fit within the autism spectrum. They suggested I get my son into the program, but the wait was *well over a year* to see a specialist or to even get a diagnosis.

Again, despair swept over me. A year's wait to get any help for my child? By then he would be starting school, and what would happen to him there? Would we ever be able to find a way to help him with the struggles he was having?

Holding back tears, I headed for the main desk where the secretary reached down and pulled out the waiting-list application for me to fill out. I asked to borrow a pen. Just then the phone beside him began to ring. I only half listened as I began filling out the form.

"You want to cancel?" the secretary asked into the receiver with disbelief. "Are you sure?"

He hung up the phone while one of the center's workers began to talk with me about the signs and symptoms of autism.

The secretary, somewhat frustrated, interrupted. "What are we going to do? We need someone to fill this spot by Tuesday. There is no way we can get someone in here that quickly!"

Suddenly, both of them turned and looked at me. "What about you? Could you fill the spot with just a few days' notice?" asked the secretary.

Goose bumps ran up and down my arm as the tension in my stomach eased. I knew I had been led to the right place at *exactly the right time*.

I accepted on the spot. One week later the center stopped taking any more names for their waiting list, saying they were overbooked. Three weeks after my prompting, my son received the diagnosis of autism by one of the leading specialists in the country.

My son began attending a social-skills group that taught him how to make eye contact, some appropriate ways to communicate with people, and the proper way to socialize in public. Along with the social group for my son, we, as parents, had the opportunity to join in a parent support group. In this group, we were able to ask questions regarding the autism spectrum and help each other solve problems.

Because my son was able to receive a definitive diagnosis, he was able to get into a special cluster unit at school to be with children that, he said, were "just like me." I will always be grateful for the prompting that came to me that day. The doors that opened at that special time in my son's life have allowed him to make great progress. Today my son is a well-adjusted middle school student in a mainstreamed school, and he is at the top of his classes.

Our trials sometimes end up helping us grow in more ways than we plan—even trials that seem unbearable. I know we have become stronger in our family, and I feel that this particular trial has led us to experience blessing upon blessing. I am especially grateful for the help we received at a time we needed it most.

Carolyn Vawdrey is the mother of five wonderful children and married to her amazing husband, Mark. She lives in the Rocky Mountains, where she enjoys writing and spending time with her family.

Whither thou goest, I will go; and
where thou lodgest, I will lodge: thy people shall
be my people, and thy God my God.

—Ruth 1:16

The Letter

by Susanne Morley

One day while I was in my own home just attending to the general affairs of the day, the thought came to me, *Sit down right now and write a letter to your sister.* This particular sister, the one just older than me, has always been my soul mate. We share philosophies and likes and dislikes. This sister has always gone out of her way for me.

The fact that I felt I should write to her was an unusual idea, though, as I've always made it a habit of getting together with her at least every two weeks. *Why the need to write a letter, then?* I decided that perhaps it was because I liked to put my thoughts down on paper, and I felt I could express myself better this way than in person. Besides, I had felt so strongly to do it that I finally just took my pen in hand and sat down to write.

In the letter I told my sister what a terrific job I thought she was doing in taking care of our mother. Our mother, who has passed on now, had lived as a widow for many years. My sister was always her constant companion. She took care of her financially, physically, and in all other ways up until the time of her death. They were like Naomi and Ruth. The words, "Whither thou goest, I will go" (Ruth 1:16) reminded me of their situation.

I continued to write that I thought she was doing a wonderful job of accomplishing her mission here on earth. I was convinced, and still am, that her special mission was to take care of our angelic mother. That was the context of my letter.

Unbeknownst to me at the time, this particular sister was going through depression. She felt like she was wasting her life, just going to her dead-end job every day and facing the same routine chores day after day.

One day when she was particularly down, she found herself waiting in a parking lot for others in her carpool to arrive to pick her up and take her to work. As she waited, she prayed earnestly inside her car. In her prayer she asked what on earth she had been born for, and what meaning did life have anyway? Especially *her* life, which she felt was so insignificant.

When she returned home after work that day, there was my letter waiting for her! I had been prompted to write it a few days earlier so it arrived *the very day* she needed it most. She told me later that she felt like it was a direct answer to prayer. After that, her spell of depression disappeared. This was as gratifying to me as having my own prayers answered. I'm grateful for the prompting that came because I love this sister dearly, and it meant a lot to me to know that the Lord would use me to help her in a way I would not have known to do on my own.

Susanne Morley is a mother and grandmother. She lives in West Valley City, Utah. A longtime member of the League of Utah Writers, Oquirrh Writers Chapter, she enjoys entering writing contests and meeting with the chapter group to critique and exchange ideas.

I will not leave you comfortless: I will come to you.

—John 14:18

Please Send Doug

by Doug Marley

After years of fighting one kind of illness after another, my wife finally met a doctor who diagnosed her with Cushing's disease. We found out that she had a tumor growing in her brain and that the only hope for recovery was considered, at best, a long shot. She would have to undergo brain surgery, and, *if she survived,* she would be bedridden for at least a year.

This was devastating news, as my wife and I had recently adopted our eighth child, making ten children in all. And our newest baby, as were most of our other children, was handicapped.

We fasted and prayed to know what to do, and after a time it became clear that there really was no other option. The tumor would continue to grow if we did not try to stop it. Our family needed a mother, and I couldn't bear the thought of losing my dearest friend, so we felt our best hope was to undergo this delicate surgery.

The day came, and amid many prayers from family and friends, a priesthood blessing, and fervent faith in our hearts, we entered the hospital. She told me that her first goal was simply to wake up in the recovery room—that is, to survive the surgery. If she even woke up after the surgery, there would be hope. As she was wheeled away, I prayed quietly for my wife to wake up in the recovery room, where I could hold her hand and help her through whatever awaited her.

I waited for hours. Night came. My wife, still breathing, was finally wheeled into the recovery room. I wanted to go to her, but hospital rules forbade visitors right after surgery. I went back to the waiting room, and as the hours passed and night deepened, I fell asleep on the couch.

Suddenly, something woke me. A strong feeling came over me that my wife needed me. Now! I quietly got up and walked down the hall. No one was in sight, and I simply opened the door to the recovery room and went in.

My wife lay there swathed in head bandages with many tubes and machines surrounding her. I placed her hand in mine, and her eyes opened.

"How did you know I needed you?" she whispered.

"I was sleeping deeply outside in the waiting room when, suddenly, I awoke and felt strongly that I needed to come to you."

"I am in so much pain," she whispered. "I have been pleading in prayer, *Please send Doug to me.* Hold my hand. Please, just hold my hand."

We held hands, and I knew she was taking strength just from my being there beside her. Although she had been heavily medicated, this kind of brain surgery was very delicate, and they had probed deeply. The pain was still intense despite all the nurses were allowed to do. But as long as I could hold her hand, she could endure it. I stayed for about twenty minutes and then slipped away again, hoping the nurses wouldn't notice.

I went back to the waiting room, and this time I dozed lightly. Suddenly, the feeling came again, and I quickly returned to my wife's room. Her pain was worse. I stayed for as long as I dared and again slipped out.

This happened three more times during the night. Each time I went back to sleep, but when my wife needed me, I awoke immediately and went to her.

We knew Heavenly Father was blessing me in this way to help and sustain my wonderful companion during one of the longest and most pain-filled nights she would ever suffer through.

Slowly, my wife recovered from that surgery. More surgeries followed, and after more years of patient suffering, she finally began to heal. Every day we have together is a great blessing, and we continue to care for our large family with gratitude that her life was spared. We feel a special appreciation that the Lord opened the way for me to bring comfort to her that one terrible night. I know that Father in Heaven is there to help us through our darkest trials.

Doug Marley works as a flight mechanic for Boeing Commercial Airplanes in Seattle, Washington. He and his wife often take their large family camping, sailing, and kayaking.

I testify . . . that the miraculous power
of divine intervention is among us, which is one of the
signs of the divinity of the work of the Lord.

—*Harold B. Lee,* Ye Are the Light of the World, *1974, 148*

The Safety Harness

by Julio Ozuna

I work in construction as a stonemason. After several months with little work, I finally got a contract to do some finish work on one of the bridges over Interstate 15, which runs through Ogden, Utah. Before beginning, we were given three hours of safety training because we would be working while traffic continued to pass us on the freeway.

My coworker, David, and I were placing decorative finish stonework on the new bridge support, which was a good thirty feet high. We began at the foot of the wall and worked upward. When we could no longer reach, we put on safety harnesses and used a truck with a mechanical lift. We would climb inside the basket and use controls there to raise and lower ourselves. It always took a few minutes to go either up or down.

Since there was federal money involved, we had a number of strict safety codes to observe. We wore our harnesses and were very careful. I wanted to please the boss because I hoped for more work. During the day, supervisors often stopped to check on us.

We wanted to finish by dark and pushed ourselves to keep working. Finally, we made the decision to return the next day since there just wasn't enough light to do well on what little remained.

The next morning we arrived and prepared to finish up the small area we had left undone the night before. I figured five or ten minutes should do it. We jumped into the basket and slowly raised ourselves to the point where we had stopped our work the night before.

Suddenly, I had words come strongly to mind: *Get down now and put on your safety harness!*

We only needed *minutes* to finish completely, and I struggled with the thought for a moment. Then, suddenly, I recalled something I had learned as a missionary. While reading the teachings of the Prophet Joseph Smith, I recalled that he once explained that a person can be much benefited when he pays attention to a prompting at the very first instance and that sometimes there won't be a second prompting, so when you hear something, act immediately.

I turned to David and said, "We need to go down now and get our safety harnesses."

He tried to argue, but I was already manning the controls to take us down. "No," I asserted. "We must go right now!"

We made it down and put on our harnesses. Then we got back into the lift, and I pushed the lever that started us back up.

Before we could reach the top, a safety inspector pulled up just below us. He got out, checked us out carefully, and inspected our work. He found everything in order.

I felt such joy inside, knowing I had listened and obeyed at the first instance! David just looked at me, suddenly understanding that we had been guided by the Spirit to put on our harnesses at that precise moment.

Yes, the work could have been completed in the short time it had taken to lower the lift, don the harnesses, and raise it again. But if we had ignored the prompting, the inspector would have arrived and caught us without our safety harnesses, and we could have been fired on the spot. We would never have been able to work for the contractor again.

I was so grateful for the remembrance that came back to me of that particular teaching of Joseph Smith. And I am grateful that the Lord helped us when I think about how it could have turned out much differently.

Julio Ozuna and his wife, Nancy, live with their family in South Jordan, Utah, where they serve faithfully in the Church. He continues to work as a stonemason.

Yea, and they did obey and
observe to perform every word of command
with exactness; yea, and even according to their
faith it was done unto them.

—Alma 57:21

Special Healing

by Cheri Chesley

One evening during my pregnancy with twins in 1999, I injured my knee. I had been sitting on the counter talking to my brother and sister-in-law, and when I got down, I hit the side of my kneecap on the edge of the counter. The soreness lasted until the bruise went away, and I didn't think of it again for a year.

The first year with twins and a two-year-old toddler catapulted hectic into a new category, especially since one of the twins was experiencing health problems. However, right around the twins' first birthday, I noticed some soreness and swelling in my knee. It became so painful that I started wearing a knee brace, and after a few months, I considered seeing a doctor. The pain kept getting worse, and I limped badly. Yet, I still had to pick up the twins at times, despite the pain, and otherwise keep up a very demanding schedule. I worried that I might need surgery, and I didn't know how to care for my young family if I was bedridden.

In May of that year, we took a road trip. At the time, we lived in Oklahoma, and we drove with the boys to visit loved ones in both Utah and Arizona. While staying with friends in Arizona, we met one of their acquaintances, a former missionary who had served in their area and had returned for a visit. My mother, who was traveling with us, asked for a priesthood blessing because she had been battling a persistent cold for several weeks. The men agreed, and we moved to a quiet room so they could perform the blessing.

As we stood in the room listening to the blessing, I heard a voice speak clearly to my mind. Warmth flooded me as the words came. *You need to ask for a blessing, and he* (the return missionary—a stranger to me) *needs to give it to you.*

The words startled me, and as they finished giving my mother a blessing, I knew I had to say something. As I did not appear sick or otherwise in need, I found myself feeling a bit shy about requesting a blessing. Still, I took my courage in hand and was obedient to the impression I had received. I asked for a blessing, and I asked that this recently returned missionary be the one to give it to me. This was awkward because not only was my husband with me but also other close family and friends, any of whom might normally have given such a blessing. Thankfully, they did not question my request. I sat in the appointed chair and folded my arms, deeply conscious of the unusual nature of what I had asked.

The blessing was short and to the point. A deep and sincere spirit flowed through this young man, which brought instant tears to my eyes. Without mentioning any of the problems I had been experiencing, he clearly commanded me to *be healed.* I was deeply touched at these words and marveled at the warmth of the Spirit that encompassed me.

That night I removed my knee brace, and from that time forward, I never put it on again.

My Heavenly Father gave me a wonderful gift that day, and I treasure the memory. Now, eight years later, occasional twinges in my knee serve as a reminder that through faith and obedience, I have been greatly blessed. I know the Lord was mindful of me at that time and not only opened a way to continue serving my young family without as much physical pain but also taught me the value of living the gospel fully every day so I can be worthy of such unexpected blessings, whenever they might be needed.

Cheri Chesley, mother of five, resides in Tooele, Utah, where she is a daycare provider, author, and Primary worker. If she had spare time, she'd enjoy reading, baking, and photography. View her website at www.cherichesley.com.

But if we hope for
that we see not, then do we with
patience wait for it.

—Romans 8:25

Ice on the Freeway

by Kelly Clark

One spring day my sister-in-law decided to travel from Orem, Utah, to St. George, Utah, to visit her parents—a five-hour drive. This was in the days before cell phones. Concerned about driving alone, she asked me to keep her company. I agreed to go with her because my four young children would enjoy spending some time with their grandparents, who also lived in St. George.

We enjoyed our visit in St. George and a few days later left for home late in the afternoon. The weather was overcast and cold. About five miles north of Fillmore, we hit an ice storm, lost control of the car, and slid off the freeway. Although other cars passing us on the freeway witnessed what had happened, no one stopped to see if we were okay.

After checking to make sure no one was hurt, we got out to assess the situation. Luckily, the only damage was a flat tire. We were able to back up onto the shoulder of the highway to try to replace the flat tire with the spare. Conditions were so icy that no one risked stopping to offer help.

Unfortunately, neither of us was strong enough to loosen the machine-tightened lug nuts. My sister-in-law offered to walk back toward Fillmore to get help, but I didn't feel like we should separate. Nor did I feel like we could hike the long distance with her. I was eight months pregnant, and the children were young. I suggested we all get back in the car and pray for safety and for help.

We agreed that this was the best option and offered a simple prayer. And then we waited . . . and waited . . . and waited. Many cars drove by, but no one stopped. After an hour, we became discouraged. I didn't know what to do and started to reconsider our options.

To our relief, a man suddenly pulled over to help and told us the following story: He explained that he had driven by about an hour earlier and had received a strong feeling then that he needed to stop but ignored the feeling. He had traveled on for another thirty minutes, but the nagging inside his mind wouldn't stop. He had finally turned around, backtracked the thirty minutes, and found us still stranded at the side of the road.

He quickly changed the tire for us, refused any kind of payment, and simply uttered regret that he had not stopped *the first time he felt impressed to do so.* We were able to drive home safely after that and will always be grateful for the man who listened to inspiration after all and went out of his way to help.

Kelly Clark is a mother of five who enjoys family life. She and her children live in Layton, Utah, where she works as a school psychologist.

Kind Understandings

For he that asketh, receiveth.

—3 Nephi 27:29

Why Me?

by Bonnie Smith

As a teacher, I decided to keep up my teaching certification, even after I married and began my family. Once I became a stay-at-home mom, I really looked forward to the certification classes. They got me out of the house for a day and gave my mind some much-appreciated professional stimulation.

One particular year I looked forward to a certain lecture series. In fact, I was quite excited by the different subjects to be covered and very much wanted to sit close to the front where I would feel I was really a part of the class. I even prayed that I could sit close to the front because I wanted to hear everything and feel the energy of the class.

But when I arrived, all the seats were taken with the exception of a few in the very back. Since I wanted so much to sit closer, I stepped inside the front door anyway and scanned the rows. I saw a woman passing out papers. When she finished, she picked up the rest of the handouts from one of the seats on the front row and left the room. I quickly slid into the seat, feeling unbelievably blessed. I had my seat up front!

I looked around at the crowd, and I silently thanked Heavenly Father for this blessing. As I did so, I also wondered, knowing that He loved all His children, why me? Why had I been so blessed to get a seat in the front of the room when there were so many others who would have liked to sit up close?

Then very clearly the words came to my mind: *Because you asked.*

This simple answer impressed me deeply. I know it was a little thing, really, and, yet, my prayer was answered. I have pondered much since that day on the blessings that we might have—if only we would ask.

Bonnie Smith and her husband, Sam, live in Kennewick, Washington, with three of their five children. The other two are attending Brigham Young University. They enjoy camping, swimming, dancing, and playing games together. They also love playing a variety of instruments together in their home.

Yea, behold, I will tell you
in your mind and in your heart, by the
Holy Ghost, which shall come upon you and
which shall dwell in your heart.

—D&C 8:2

I Expected a Vision

by María Serafini de Ozuna

When I was twenty-eight years old, my husband and I lived with other family members in our home in Paraguay. My brother noticed two young men who passed our house from time to time. He wanted to know who they were and what they taught.

One day he finally motioned for them to stop. They came in and began giving my brother the missionary lessons. He was baptized a month later.

My brother was very excited about this new religion and invited my husband and me to listen to the elders. We said we would, and we began the missionary lessons. I learned about Joseph Smith, who seemed like a very young person to be starting a church and translating records, especially if he only had a third-grade education. Besides, I was very active in my own church.

Out of curiosity, I read the entire Book of Mormon. Could Joseph Smith have really translated this? The missionaries, of course, assured me that it was not only possible but that it had also happened just as they had taught us. Then they told us that we needed to fast as well as pray about it, and the Spirit would confirm it to us.

I decided to try this. If the Spirit was going to confirm it, then it seemed to me that I would have a vision. Or maybe a dream. Something of significance.

I began to fast and pray to know if the Book of Mormon was true, if Joseph Smith was a prophet, and if a young man with only a third-grade education could have really translated a work like that.

Then I waited for my vision. Hours passed. Nothing happened.

The missionaries visited us that night, and I explained that I had not received a vision or dream or anything at all.

"No, no," explained one of the elders. "Your answer won't come like that. You will feel it—in your mind and in your heart."

The next morning, still fasting, I went to work. While tending the store, I pondered on the things I had prayed about. Suddenly, a great joy filled me. In my *mind,* I knew it was all true, and in my *heart,* I felt great happiness. It filled all of my being, and to this day, I still recall the tremendous joy that enveloped me.

I saw the missionaries approaching, and one called out to me, "Sister Ozuna, did you get your answer?"

"Yes!" I exclaimed. "I feel such happiness."

"Are you ready to get baptized?" he asked.

I wanted to say yes, but I wanted my husband to get baptized with me. "Let's talk to my husband," I said.

It took eight months, but at last my husband was also ready for baptism. Together we entered the baptismal waters, and we have been firm and faithful members of the Church ever since.

I am grateful for the unmistakable witness I received from the Spirit that day. No, I didn't have a vision. But I had an experience that touched the very center of my soul, and I knew it was true.

María Ozuna and her husband, Feliciano, have five children and five grandchildren. They joined the Church five years after they were married and have remained strong in the Church ever since. All of their children are faithful members, serving missions and marrying in the temple.

And now behold, I say unto you, my brethren, if ye have experienced a change of heart, and if ye have felt to sing the song of redeeming love, I would ask, can ye feel so now?

—Alma 5:26

Not Anthony!

by L. T. Elliot

I was seventeen years old when my parents took us to meet Anthony. He was a small, dark-haired, dark-eyed boy just shy of eight years. Anthony and his younger sister were currently living with some family friends of ours who also happened to be foster parents. When my mother and father first told us about the camping trip, I had no reason to suspect that it might be anything other than a normal, friendly visit with people we'd loved for a long time.

I can't recall the exact moment my parents told us they were thinking about adopting Anthony, but I'll never forget how I felt. Waves of bitter anger washed over me, leaving tinges of guilt and uncertainty in their wake. I spent the remainder of the journey up the mountainside in alternating frenzies of fury and helplessness. I was number five of seven children and currently the oldest child at home. Why did they need more? I remembered thinking that my parents didn't even have enough time and love for *me*. How could they possibly think about adopting *another* child?

There was plenty of daylight left when we reached camp, leaving us ample time to get acquainted with the little interloper. Oh, sure, he was cute enough, with eyes like melted milk chocolate, smooth dark skin, and a smile that embodied childish glee. But he would be just one more seat at a family table that already felt too squished. Every time I looked at him, I felt like I watched my parents' divided affection swirling that much further away from me.

I couldn't make myself warm up to him.

Worse, my younger brother and Anthony hit it off instantly, running and screeching through the camp, playing mock battles with broken sticks, and ducking through bushes. I spent my time avoiding them and hanging around with Rachel, a girl my own age. My mom and Anthony's foster mother clucked like chickens in a farmyard, catching up on all the time since they had last seen each other.

Dinner came and went, and before long everyone was talking about the business of sleeping arrangements. I'd always assumed I'd sleep in my parents' motor home and hadn't even thought of bringing a sleeping bag. It was around this time that my dad picked up on my moody signals and thought he'd have a talk with me. He asked me what had been bothering me all day. Running out of evasions, I finally confessed my feelings about their decision to adopt. He looked taken aback.

"Laura, we've always raised our children to be open to adoption. We almost adopted that little boy Taylor, and you didn't say anything then," my dad pointed out.

I hung my head, trying to avoid my father's eyes. "But it fell through. It never seemed like it was real. Not like this time."

I didn't need to see my dad's face to know he was disappointed. I could feel it emanating from him. "Your mom and I have always believed that the Lord never limits the human heart, that there aren't restrictions to how much love a person can share with others. Adopting Anthony would be no different than if your mom was pregnant with another baby."

"I wouldn't want another baby, either!" I couldn't help crying out. "You guys hardly love the kids you've got. What makes you think you can love one more? How is that fair to this little boy, let alone your *real kids*?" I asked him, wiping away hot streaks of shaming tears.

My dad looked at me for a moment, his eyes focused on mine. I couldn't tell what was going through his mind, but I felt the weight of his accusing stare and finally ripped my gaze away, unable to face him anymore.

"I really think you need to pray about this, Laura. I think that when you turn to your Heavenly Father, you'll see that not only do your mother and I love you, but that we also have enough love for all our children as well as for one more child who really needs it."

My father didn't give me much of a choice. He told me that I'd be sleeping in Rachel's tent, and it just so happened that Anthony would be sharing it with us. I didn't want to share with them and tried everything I could to get my dad to change his mind, but he insisted. I was stuck.

I remember crawling into the tent, devoid of everything but a pillow, and laying my stuff down as close to Rachel as I could get. Maybe she'd let me share a blanket with her, since there was no way I was going back to fight with my dad again.

Rachel and I talked for a while, listened to music, and swapped tales of things we'd been up to lately, but before long it was time for bed. I tried to do what my dad had asked, to pray to see if what he said was true. Would my Father in Heaven really change my heart? Could He really make me feel any different than I did? So I prayed.

Nothing changed. I still felt as upset and angry as I'd ever been.

I curled up on my side, punching my pillow in frustration. How could I be so jealous of an eight-year-old? It wasn't fair that he could just walk in and claim my parents' affection when I had spent years trying to earn it and still felt like I'd never have it. How could my parents ask this of me? It wasn't fair.

I tried to sleep. I wanted to block it out of my head and just let the oblivion of dreams take over, whisking me away from all my jealous, heartsore feelings. I wanted to pretend we never came to this stupid mountain, but I was so cold that sleep evaded me. Every time I relaxed just enough to surrender to sleep, my own shivering would wake me, and the discomfort of my chilled skin kept me awake.

When I felt something drape over my bare arms, I jumped and sat up. I turned hastily, seeing Anthony standing over me with a startled expression and his hands outstretched as though he'd just dropped something. I looked down to see a ragged, threadbare blanket covering me—a child's blanket, not even big enough to cover my legs. It had the look of something that had been loved and used often.

"What are you doing, Anthony?" I turned to him, asking him in a harsh whisper.

His little dark eyes looked black and shiny. "You were shivering. I thought you were cold, so I gave you my blanket."

I craned my head to look at his little bed. There was only a pillow left. "You don't have to do that, Anthony. You need this blanket. I'll be all right."

He shook his head, that infectious smile spreading over his face. "No, I'm okay. You're cold." And he turned to go back to his little pillow.

Shock, cold and clear, slapped me. All this time I'd been thinking I was so poorly done by. I didn't want to share my parents with anyone, yet this little boy who didn't know me at all shared literally everything he had with me.

I clutched the little threadbare blanky to my chest, tears filling my eyes. I could feel my heart yielding. God hadn't refused to answer my prayer; He just couldn't reach me through my own selfishness. I might have prayed for understanding, but I didn't let Him in. I had refused to listen. Suddenly, I wasn't the kid my parents didn't love enough; I was the girl who didn't know how to love enough. And Anthony had just showed me how much I had to learn.

"How about we share it?" I called out.

Anthony stopped and turned to look back at me, that darling smile in place again. "Sure!"

He grabbed his pillow and ran back to snuggle up between Rachel and me. The difference in the spirit in our tent was notable. I fell asleep thinking that the best example of true love and kindness I'd ever learned had been taught to me by an eight-year-old boy with a tattered old blanket.

The next morning I woke up to a whole new attitude. Only Rachel had known what Anthony had done, but everyone could see the difference it had made in my behavior toward him. Where jealousy had once grown rampant, love bloomed instead. It was as fixed as anything I felt toward my own little brother, and I knew it had changed me forever.

Shortly after that camping trip, my mother was diagnosed with multiple sclerosis, and the doctor would not give the "all clear" for Anthony's adoption, fearing that my mom's health would be too taxed to raise another child. It was a devastating blow to our family for many reasons, not the least of which was the loss of Anthony as our little brother.

I asked God why He would bless me with this overwhelming love for this little boy when He must have known that we would never get to call Anthony our own.

Anthony and his little sister were both adopted by their foster parents and have a permanent home with them. Even though he was not ours officially, Anthony has called my mom "Mother" and has remained close to our family for years. He addresses each letter to my parents as "Mom & Dad," and every chance we have had to spend with him is precious to us.

Over the years, I have asked myself why God would have shown me how to open my heart to another sibling only to have him taken away, and I have discovered that it wasn't a cosmic answer about adoption. The truth is I didn't get a simple answer. My Heavenly Father just opened my eyes to see the goodness in Anthony's heart. It had always been there—I had just been too caught up in myself to see it. Anthony taught me one of the most valuable lessons I've ever learned—that the divine is in every human heart, that every soul is worth loving, and that my heart has room enough to embrace more than I imagined.

I will never forget the lesson he taught me or the love I still feel for Anthony. I will always treasure the moment a darling little boy wrapped me up in his tattered blanket and claimed a part of my heart that is all his own.

L. T. Elliot lives in the western United States. She spends most of her time playing with her kids, hanging out with family, and escaping to worlds within her mind. You can learn more about her at www.lixiconluvr.blogspot.com.

Be thou humble; and the Lord thy
God shall lead thee by the hand, and give
thee answer to thy prayers.

—D&C 112:10

Where Was Andrew?

by Michael S. Eldredge

In 1976 I was a lieutenant in the Navy and was stationed in California. I was assigned to attend a seminar at the Naval Academy in Annapolis, Maryland. I decided that at the conclusion of the seminar, I would take the opportunity to drive to my mother's birthplace in north-central Missouri.

Though I had grown up in Ogden, Utah, as a Presbyterian, I was a descendant on my father's side of several Mormon pioneers, including Orson Pratt and Joseph Underwood Eldredge, both pioneers with the 1847 group.

My mother's family, however, was a different matter. Along with my grandmother, Lula Scott Decker, Mother came to Utah from Iowa during World War II. She told me a number of so-called facts about the family—that I was a descendant of Daniel Boone and that the Deckers and the Scotts had been on opposite sides in the Civil War. True or not, I didn't know. She also taught me to say "Mizzora," not "Mizzooreee!"

I was baptized into The Church of Jesus Christ of Latter-day Saints just a year before my mother passed away. I was nineteen at the time, married, and had a son. As I learned more about the teachings of the Church, I became aware of the importance of family history. So a few years later, when I decided to make the stop in Missouri, I wanted to go prepared. I gathered what information I could find from various relatives, including the name of a great-aunt in her eighties, Sylvia Scott, who still lived in the area.

I arrived in Kirksville, Missouri, late in the evening and immediately went to my great-aunt Sylvia's house. As I stood on her front porch at ten o'clock in the evening, it occurred to me that an elderly woman might not want to talk to a stranger at this time of night! I turned to leave just as the door opened. Surprised, I stammered, "I know you don't know me, but my grandmother was . . ."

She had a quizzical look on her face. "Michael?" she said, breaking into my introduction.

I was astonished that she knew me. As it turned out, she knew my face from an old newspaper clipping my grandmother had sent her when I received my Eagle Scout award.

She asked me in and seemed thrilled to see me. Nothing had prepared me for such a warm reception or for the amount of information about my ancestors I received over the next hour. We arranged to meet again with her daughter, my cousin Maxine, who would show me various family history sites. As I started to leave, I turned to Aunt Sylvia and asked her if she had a picture of my grandmother when she was young.

She smiled, and with a twinkle in her eye, said, "Wait just a minute," and disappeared into the other room. When she returned, she held a small photograph album in her hands and placed it in my lap. "This belonged to your grandmother, and you should have it."

I opened the album and found it to be a photographic record of my grandmother's years as a young woman before she was married. I was at a total loss for words.

When I arrived to meet my cousin Maxine on Sunday afternoon, I knew that one primary focus of my trip would be to search for my great-great-grandfather, Andrew Scott. Andrew was the grandfather of Great-aunt Sylvia's husband, Jasper Scott. He had arrived in Adair County in the 1850s and had married Mary Bailey in 1859. I had obtained the marriage date of Andrew and Mary Bailey through the Church's Temple Record Index Bureau, reflecting ordinances done based on extracted records. There was no record, however, of Andrew's birth or death date, so I hoped I would find his grave. Maxine told me that an old family tradition held that Andrew was buried near the original farm where my grandmother was born and grew up. The Scott family still owned the property, so we headed over there.

Our first stop was the old farmhouse, which was no longer in use but still had all the original furnishings inside, covered in sheets. I felt a tie to the place—that it was an important anchor in my life. After a brief walk around the house looking for a possible grave site, Maxine took me to several local cemeteries where I recorded names and dates. Our last stop was the Ft. Madison cemetery, not far from the old farm.

"If Grandpa Andrew is buried in any cemetery, it is probably here," she commented as we strolled through the rows of old headstones. Maxine started at one end and I at the other, making a quick visual check of headstones. The sun was low, shining through the branches of trees across the road. Many of the headstones were worn and illegible. I walked slowly, trying to decipher the words on each. As I walked slowly down a row in the northwest section of the cemetery, I heard a still, quiet voice say, *Stop!*

Startled, I looked around. I could see no one except Maxine several rows away. I was standing next to a lone grave marker that had apparently been broken, then jammed back into the earth. Curious, I bent down, loosened it, and pulled it out. The inscription read "Eliza, wife of A. Scott." There were no dates engraved on the stone. Puzzled, I gently replaced the stone marker. I was looking for a Mary, not an Eliza. Nevertheless, I pulled a piece of scrap paper from my pocket, wrote down the epitaph and location, folded it, and stuck it in my wallet. Neither Maxine nor I found any other gravestones that appeared related to our ancestors.

The next morning, Monday, I arrived at the Adair County Courthouse at eight o'clock sharp. Though I had obtained a substantial amount of information over the weekend, I knew that I needed to verify dates from official records. I also hoped that by some stroke of luck I might find information about Andrew Scott.

I was very excited when the clerk brought me the first big binder of the county's oldest records. As I eagerly opened it, I suddenly felt a cold, dark chill sweep over me. Looking at the pages, I was amazed to see that I could not read any of the writing. The letters looked like strange symbols and were completely unintelligible to me. I blinked, trying to dispel the darkness and confusion before me. The clerk was watching me and asked if anything was wrong. Realizing that I was face to face with some adversarial opposition, I closed the book and slid it back to the clerk, telling her I would return in a few moments.

Outside on the courthouse steps, I sat in the sun and thought about what had just happened, awed at the manifestation of opposition that I had sensed. I rebuked the evil spirit and returned to the clerk's office. This time I could read the writing easily. I spent the next three hours copying dates and names, filling in almost all of the holes in my records. But I found no record of Andrew.

I spent the afternoon organizing all of my data. I decided to take a quick nap before dinner. Just as I was dozing off, I awoke with a start. I had a strong impression to return to the old farmhouse.

I asked permission to visit the house again, and within minutes I was headed north. I came to a stop near the farm. The old house was directly across the road and down a gentle hill. The sun was low in the west, shining through the trees, with long shadows reaching out to surround the farmhouse. I walked to the door and let myself in. Inside, it was very still. In the cellar, I saw jars of unopened fruit put up on the dusty shelves decades ago.

As I slowly wandered through the house, I thought it might be nice to take back a souvenir of my trip. Entering a bedroom, I noticed an old postcard sitting on a dresser. As I looked closer, I saw that it was a picture of the courthouse where I had spent the morning. Turning it over, I noted that it was postmarked at 10:30 AM on August 1, 1925. My mother's birthday! Eagerly I read:

Dear brothers,
had a 9 lb girl arrive at 4 o'clock this morning, her name
is Bonnie Lou, are getting along fine. Please let us no [sic]
how you all are. Love to all Lou

Bonnie Lou was my mother. Stunned, I felt chills run up and down my spine as I read the announcement of my mother's birth written in my grandmother's hand. I wondered if my grandmother was nearby and had meant for me to have this. If so, the post card was perhaps the most precious gift she could have given me that day. I felt that my finding it was not an accident.

I later returned home to California with my treasured information. Two years later I was a first-year law student at BYU, studying, among other subjects, real property law. On the day we learned about dower interests, something clicked. I came home and rummaged through my genealogy files, eventually finding the note I had written at the Ft. Madison cemetery.

The next day I cut classes and headed for the genealogy library to look at Adair County land records. There, I found Andrew's trail through the dower releases of Eliza Jane Riggs, *his first wife who died in 1858.* I realized that the A. Scott listed on Eliza's gravestone that day was likely a reference to my grandfather, Andrew! But I still didn't know where he was buried or anything more about him. I tracked him into Des Moines County, Iowa, then to Adair County. I was ecstatic, but from there, the trail again went cold.

Several years later, in June 1989, I was in the Family History Library in Salt Lake City, Utah, and came across a surname index for Iowa. Browsing through the index, I found an entry for all of my Des Moines County Scott ancestors. I looked up the submitter's name and quickly wrote a letter to her.

No response ever came, and after a couple of years I forgot about the letter. Then, on November 18, 1993, I received a letter that began, "Dear Michael Scott Eldredge, please be there yet!"

As I read through her letter, I discovered the writer was a cousin descended from Andrew by his first wife Eliza. She wrote about my ancestor, Mary Bailey, who, I learned, had been twice widowed before she married Andrew. Her maiden name was Scott, also from Ohio. I quickly got on the phone with her, and we talked for two hours. Just as I was about to hang up, I asked her, almost in passing, if she knew where Andrew was buried.

"Oh, yes," she replied. "He's buried in the Ft. Madison Cemetery next to his first wife, Eliza, and your grandma, Mary, is buried on the other side of him. I don't think there are headstones on Andrew's or Mary's grave, but there is on Eliza's."

At a loss for words, I thanked her and told her I would call again.

I was stunned. I had, after all, stood by both Mary and Andrew's graves that day. Emotion gripped me as I realized my ancestors were aware of me and my great desire to find where they were buried and had led me to the exact spot with the quiet command, *Stop!*

I realize that our bonds to eternity are many and strong. No matter what distractions may exist, there are keys to every door that we encounter on the paths we follow to find our ancestors. I was fortunate to "hear" a simple message at a brief moment in an otherwise incredibly busy weekend. And I treasure the simple gift of an old postcard that has anchored my testimony of the importance and divinity of this work.

As for Daniel Boone, it turns out that my grandmother was right, or at least almost right. I discovered my great-grandmother was, in fact, a niece of Daniel. But then, that's another story.

Mike Eldredge is a 1980 graduate of the J. Reuben Clark Law School at Brigham Young University. He and his wife, Michelle, reside in Salt Lake City. They have eight children and eleven grandchildren.

*And it came to pass
that I beheld a tree, whose fruit was
desirable to make one happy.*

—1 Nephi 8:10

My Uncle's Dream

by José Angel Seferino Raya y Gonzales

Many years ago in my native home of Mexico, my uncle became very ill, and it was clear that he would soon pass away. Relatives gathered at his bedside, crying and mourning his passing. I was only a child at the time, but I felt very sad about my uncle.

Then, without warning, my uncle rallied a bit and told everyone to stop crying. He tried to explain something to us—something he seemed to be experiencing. I watched, both puzzled and curious. He appeared calm, even happy as he struggled to tell us that there were people beckoning him . . . but they were across a river.

As my uncle talked, the room quieted.

Then, he said he saw an iron rod and told us he was going to grasp it. When he took hold of the rod, he explained that there was a beautiful white tree ahead of him. He wanted to go toward it.

We listened, spellbound. We had never before heard of anyone describing such scenes, especially on their deathbed. And we had certainly never heard of rivers, iron rods, and trees. It was very strange to all of us.

My uncle passed away soon after, but his unusual words left a deep impression upon me. Years passed, and I married and raised a family. The day came that I traveled to the United States to see if I could better our economic situation. I went to work as a painter in Salt Lake City, Utah. My boss, also from Mexico, was a member of the Church.

My circumstances were such that I needed a place to stay. My boss suggested that his parents might be able to rent me a room. I moved in with Brother and Sister Bellazetín.

This couple began telling me about The Church of Jesus Christ of Latter-day Saints, and they gave me a copy of the Book of Mormon. I began to read, and almost immediately, I read the story of Lehi and his dream. I couldn't believe it! It reflected almost exactly what my dying uncle had been trying to describe.

Intrigued, I went to church on Sunday. In class, I stood and introduced myself. I said I hoped there was someone who might tell me more about the Church because I was thinking about joining. I didn't notice the big grin on the faces of two young men sitting in the Gospel Principles class with me.

But that very afternoon they came to the house, and I began taking the missionary discussions. Within a short time, they invited me to be baptized. I accepted everything they were saying—I deeply felt a witness that it was true. Yet, I was feeling suddenly rushed. Was this the right thing to do? My wife was still in Mexico. Should I wait until I returned so I could talk to her? I needed more time to think about it.

That Friday night, when the elders stopped in, I told them I wasn't ready to be baptized on Sunday. Later on, I went to bed, praying to know the truth and what I should do.

I fell asleep and had a dream. In the dream, I saw a temple with many people standing outside, welcoming me. They were dressed in white and looked happy. And standing among all those people was Brother Bellazetín, his face aglow.

I awoke and knew I'd received my answer. That Sunday I was baptized. My uncle, who had passed away many years earlier, had led me to the truth! I knew the Lord was watching over our family and had opened this door for us.

Angel Raya continues to live and work in Utah and looks forward to the day when his wife can join him. In the meantime, he is busy introducing the gospel to other family members. Some of them have recently joined the Church.

*For he will give unto the faithful
line upon line, precept upon precept.*

—D&C 98:12

Two-way Help

Name Withheld

During the early years of my marriage, I was often overcome with feelings of disappointment that my relationship with my husband wasn't very strong. In fact, as time continued, I grew apprehensive whenever we had to be together for any length of time. I wasn't enjoying life, my children, or my marriage. It seemed to be all work and no fun.

Was this normal? I wondered often how anyone is supposed to know what is considered normal and what is not. I talked guardedly to a few friends, trying to figure out if most wives went through times of misery and unhappiness. One of my friends assured me that she, too, had had exaggerated ideas of wedded bliss, but with the years she had just lowered her expectations to a more realistic level and found that as she did so, she felt better about her husband and the marriage.

I thought about that and decided I'd been basically duped by Hollywood and the whole happily-ever-after concept. Marriage was hard work—a lot of it.

But I was so unhappy. Eventually, not knowing where to turn, I felt that only my Heavenly Father could help me understand what was going on and if things could change. I prayed with great fervor, seeking help, begging for understanding.

Slowly, over a very long period of time, principles came. I tried each one as it was taught to me and felt I had gained insight and taken a step for the better. But they were such tiny steps! However, another year would go by, and I'd learn something else.

Finally, I came to the point where I had learned a few concepts that were basic to improving our marital difficulties. I was becoming much more knowledgeable about human relationships.

About that time Elder Richard G. Scott of the Quorum of the Twelve visited our area. He had been my mission president years earlier, and I was delighted to renew our acquaintance. In the course of our conversation, he told me of a mission reunion that was to take place in Salt Lake City, Utah, at the next general conference. I decided to go to Utah and attend both the reunion and general conference.

The reunion was rewarding, and I saw several friends I hadn't seen since my days in the mission field. The next day, Saturday, Elder Scott spoke in the afternoon session of conference. I took paper and pencil and sat taking copious notes during his remarks. First, he mentioned one of the concepts I'd been taught by the Lord some time earlier. *Yes, I thought, that's so true!* A few minutes later, he mentioned another concept I'd been taught. *Why, yes. Exactly!* Again, I had the feeling of hearing familiar truth.

He continued with his talk, and by the end, he'd covered every one of the concepts I felt I had learned through great prayer, longing, seeking, and suffering. The problem was he was talking to women in abusive relationships! Why . . . how could that be? My husband didn't hit me. Yet . . . these were the identical principles I had been taught through study and prayer. So that meant . . . I was, indeed, in an abusive relationship.

Shock settled upon me. It was like seeing truth for the first time. I pondered this new knowledge in my heart, contemplating what it meant for me.

After visiting with friends, I headed back to where I was staying. It was getting late, and the Saturday priesthood session had just ended. As I drove along the freeway, I thought, *I wish I could talk to Elder Scott.* Immediately, I felt a strong impression reverberate inside me: *Call him!*

Shock went through me. I was just a homemaker; he was an Apostle. The fact that I'd just attended a missionary reunion didn't give me special privileges, and I was pretty sure he wouldn't want a million women calling him up. But . . . the impression was so clear I knew I would have to call him.

When I got back to the place I was staying, with my hand shaking, I dialed his number. And when he answered, for the first time in my life, I admitted I was living in a verbally abusive relationship. My voice shook, and it was difficult to admit out loud. And then I said, "Elder Scott, I have had a personal witness that the things you said tonight are true. I've been taught these very principles through fasting and prayer over the last few years. I know what you said is correct. Thank you."

We chatted and then hung up. I felt good. I'd done as I'd been impressed to do, and the chat, though brief, had been sympathetic and satisfying.

The following morning headlines blared on TV, the radio, and in the newspaper about his comments, suggesting he didn't have a clue about abuse problems or was himself hiding a guilty conscience. Activist groups had marched to the Tabernacle to picket in protest. I was shocked.

And then I recalled the strong impression I had had the night before to call him. During that call I had borne a strong witness—a witness from a faithful Latter-day Saint woman—that the words he spoke were true. He needed to hear that witness first, *that very night,* so that when the furor broke in the morning, he could be sustained with the knowledge that the faithful sisters of the Church would know he spoke the truth.

For me, having finally put a label on the problem, I was able to get some help. My husband was shocked to find out his words were considered abusive. Change began, and today we are still married and finally living in peace. I know that the Lord led us through, line upon line, precept upon precept, to get where we are today. And somehow, by being willing to go through that difficult process, I feel I was able to be of comfort to a member of the Quorum of the Twelve.

*Counsel with the Lord
in all thy doings, and he will direct
thee for good.*

—Alma 37:37

Why Him?

by Anna del C. Dye

It was early December on a bright morning in the town of Peña Blanca, Chile. I was nineteen years old and traveling to the city, one hour from my home, for my internship as a professional seamstress. I sat quietly on the train when I noticed the cute young man in a dark suit who sat across from me with a black book in his hand. This was the same scene I had witnessed now for the past three weeks. I was curious about the clean-cut young man who sat reading the book and pondering quietly. Each day my interest in him increased. However, this day would be different.

When I returned home from school that day, I was informed that my cousin, who was living in another town, would be getting married in a Mormon chapel in our town. I had no idea what a Mormon was, but my aunt asked my sisters and me to take turns accompanying her other daughter, who would be here for a long visit, to various church meetings until the bride arrived. As none of us was a member, she felt that some of us ought to attend for a while, especially if we hoped to use the chapel for a wedding.

One night it was my turn to go to something called Mutual, and to my astonishment, the cute young man from the train was there! I found out he was the Young Men president, and he kissed my cheek when we were introduced, as is customary in Chile. Wow. I had no problem going to all the meetings after that, even if I still didn't know what Mormons were.

Three weeks later, after the missionaries had started teaching my cousin and me the discussions, we were introduced to something called family home evening. The event was to take place at my aunt's home on a Saturday evening. All the young people from the branch attended, including the enchanting young man . . . and his steady girlfriend. What a letdown!

I had never felt so foolish in my whole life. He had a steady girlfriend, and I didn't even know it. Well, that night I went home and thought of how silly I had been. Somewhere in my disappointment, I wished that the next young man I thought I was falling in love with would be the one I actually married! I knew it was just a reaction, but that's what went through my mind that night.

So I went to stake conference the next day, somewhat determined to find a nice, clean-cut young man who might be someone I could one day love. It was a very uplifting meeting, but the scenes from the previous night kept returning to my mind more often than I wanted because of the deep shame that came with them.

"How foolish I was," I kept repeating to myself.

When conference ended, we all got on a bus to return to our hometown. I soon noticed that the object of my recent affections was taking the same bus. He kissed every girl's cheek, as was the custom, and soon stopped at my side. He noticed that I was quiet and asked me what the matter was.

I thought it was funny that he would ask me such a question. So I summoned my courage and answered that there was this boy I liked . . . but he had a steady girlfriend. He looked at me and said, without taking a breath, "You need to pray and ask if he is your eternal companion. If he is, then something will happen, and he will return to your side."

I smiled politely while my inner voice thought, *Prayer? Yeah, right.* Although I had been praying for a couple of weeks by then, I still had a hard time coming up with things that I could ask for or give thanks for. I got red-faced and empty-headed every time I tried. And answers to prayer . . . well, that hadn't yet happened, either. So his words seemed useless.

Still, his answer stayed with me all day. After I had said a small prayer that night and had jumped in bed, I thought it over. Pray to know whom to marry? A moment later I threw back the covers, knelt on the bed, and began by addressing our Heavenly Father. Then I paused, trying to form my thoughts. *Tomorrow* . . . I stopped. The thought that came to me was that I would see the man I was to marry early the next day! That was not what I had intended to say.

Embarrassment flooded me. I quickly closed the prayer and dropped flat on my bed and covered my head with the blanket. I felt my face catch on fire all the way to my ears. What kind of a prayer was that? Where had such words come from? They surprised even me.

After my heart returned to normal, I thought about the strange thought that had come to me and how impossible it would be for it to come true. For starters, it wasn't my turn to do the shopping, so there was no way I would get out of the house the next day. Therefore, I would not be seeing any young men at all. I finally shrugged and fell asleep. This prayer thing was very new to me, and I obviously wasn't doing it right.

The next morning the beautiful sounds of birds woke me up just as the sun started to bathe our window in light. No one was up yet, and my twin sister slept peacefully in the bed next to mine. As I surveyed the bright colors of the walls in my room, seemingly for the first time, a beautiful feeling of peace overcame me, and the image of one of the missionaries who was teaching me the discussions came strongly to mind.

As I pondered in wonder, I thought back to the night before and my poor attempt to pray. But this couldn't possibly be connected . . . could it? I didn't even like him much. He was just another elder. *So . . . why him?* I wondered. *Besides, he isn't even from here. He will leave, and I will never see him again.*

Yet, from that day on I experienced an upwelling of emotion whenever I thought about what had taken place that morning. I didn't know what to make of it. I wondered often, *Could it be real?* Yet the more I thought about it, the happier I felt. Something very warm bathed my senses, and I couldn't stop smiling. My attitude toward the young man was changing, but I wasn't sure that was wise. I knew by then that missionaries didn't date and decided again that he would likely leave in a few weeks, and that would be that.

The following Sunday everything was fine—until I saw this young elder smile at me from the bench where he sat. By then both my cousin and I had been baptized, *and* I had been called to serve as the Sunday School secretary. In those days we used to sit up front, and from my seat I could not help but watch him. But the more I did, the more I felt heat rise to my face. I was sure everyone in the room was staring at me.

Later that week, the same missionary greeted me at church and passed chocolate kisses to me in his handshake. I wondered why he had chosen me for his gift. He merely explained that his mother had sent him the treats, and those were his last. I didn't know the name of them, so I thought nothing about it then.

Three weeks went by. I was home one day when my father and younger sister came home at 12:30 PM and told me that the elder had been transferred and would be leaving on the 1:00 PM train to Santiago, the capital of my country.

I would likely never see him again, and I wondered again about the image of him that had come to me in my room that morning. I suddenly felt that I needed to pray.

I retired to the quietest room in my house and there offered another prayer. *Please,* I said, *if he is to be my eternal companion, let me see him one last time.* I was so inexperienced at praying that I wasn't sure if that was proper, but I had done the best I could to obey the idea that had come to my mind.

With mixed feelings, I got ready for Relief Society later that day. He was surely gone, and I hadn't seen him. So . . . ? What did it all mean?

At 3:30 PM I started my walk toward our chapel. There were two routes I could take to arrive at the meetinghouse, and when I got to the fork in the road, I had a feeling that I should go the way that went by my bishop's house.

When I got to the bishop's house, I stopped by the door just as the blond, blue-eyed missionary came out, almost knocking me down! My surprise was complete. I stood rooted to the ground. How could it be possible that he was still here?

He apologized for scaring me. We talked a little, and then he said that he needed to get his luggage to catch the train at 4:00 PM. He extended his hand to me and kept it a bit longer than necessary. "I am glad we got to say good-bye," he said. Then he left.

But I had seen him once more. I kept these feelings close to my heart and went on with my life, unsure what to make of it but leaving it to the Lord.

Two weeks later I received a letter from him! In it he said that this would be the only letter I was to receive from him, for it was against the rules for a missionary to write to a girl while in the mission field but that he had asked permission to write me this once. He told me of his love for the Lord and his mission. Then he encouraged me to learn English, to stay faithful in the Church, and to prepare to go to the temple one day. He promised to write me when his mission ended.

I began to take a deeper interest in learning to speak English and in living the gospel. Over a year later, I did, indeed, hear again from the young man.

It has been thirty-three years since that time, and, needless to say, the young missionary I didn't like has become my beloved eternal companion. Two weeks before we were married, we shared with each other what we each had experienced during the time he worked in my town. It turned out that each of us had received a special witness from the Spirit during the weeks he was assigned to my hometown; otherwise, we might never have seen each other again.

We live in Utah now, and three boys and a girl have joined our eternal family. I know that the Lord brought us together in a way that strengthened us for all that would follow, because I would need to leave my beloved homeland and live in a new country.

With my beloved's total support and the Spirit as a guide, I have been able to blossom and develop many talents I could not have developed in my native country. Also, I have been given the honor of working in the house of the Lord as a temple worker, and I have been given the opportunity to spread the values of the gospel through the books I write.

As I think back on that time when offering personalized prayers was such a new concept to me, I learned that it really was possible to speak my heart to God . . . and that He would lead me to know what was true through the power of the Spirit—including whom I should marry.

Anna del C. Dye is mother of four and foster mother of forty. She serves as a temple worker and has worked as a theatrical costumer. She also enjoys writing books about medieval teen fantasy. You can visit her website at www.annadelc.com.

The gift of God is eternal life through Jesus Christ our Lord.

—Romans 6:23

Where Is His Gift?

by Sergey Preobrashensky, as told to Helen Glissmeyer

Christmas was something new for me and my family after we immigrated to the United States from the Soviet Union. We had never celebrated that holiday in our native country. Instead, we celebrated New Year's Day when Grandpa Frost brought presents to put under the tree.

I will never forget our first Christmas in America. It was terrible. We lived in Boston, Massachusetts, at that time. Because we had never celebrated Christmas, we didn't know anything about it. We found all the people around us seemingly struggling with many things to do and prepare. Many of them seemed to be suffering. They did not seem to be enjoying themselves. No one seemed especially happy, and the customs seemed strange and hard to comprehend. Although it was often spoken of as a season of joy, we could not see why.

By the time we decided to do our best to mark this new holiday, it was Christmas Eve. My wife, Marina, and I went out shopping to find gifts for our children, but all the stores were closed. This surprised us. Frustrated, we eventually bought a few things at a gas station and went home. It was not a good time for us.

The day after Christmas my wife came home with a Christmas tree, fully decorated. She was excited because she had bought it for a good price. It had been in a store window on display, and the store was now getting rid of it. Imagine that! Our family used the tree to celebrate the New Year, just like we had done in Moscow.

Two years later our Christmas was much different.

My wife and I had grown up in Moscow in atheist families, but somehow we came to believe that God did exist. We lived in the Soviet

Union until after we had three children. While we were there, we started to look for the true church where our family could worship together. We had a feeling that we should go to the United States. We didn't know why, but we seemed to know there was a reason for us to go there.

We first heard about The Church of Jesus Christ of Latter-day Saints in Ladispoli, Italy, a city near Rome. We had to go there to wait for our immigration papers to be processed before we could enter the United States. A friend of mine, also from Moscow, invited me to play soccer with him and some "very strange American men." He thought they must be CIA agents because they were so young, so busy, and were always dressed in white shirts and ties.

As I played soccer with these four men, I learned that they were missionaries of the Church. I was impressed by how they treated each other, showing love and kindness. After the game, two of them asked if they could come to our home to visit us.

When we talked to the two missionaries in our home, we liked them very much and tried to find out about their families and how they grew up. They came to see us several times, but we didn't join the Church at that time.

After arriving in the United States, we continued to search for a church for our family and investigated several of them. Sometimes I even attended two different churches on one Sunday. During our search, I came across The Church of Jesus Christ of Latter-day Saints once again. But at first I wasn't sure it was what we were looking for.

However, I had a deep desire to investigate more.

We began to attend meetings of the Church, but because we came from another country, it was difficult for us. Although my wife and I spoke some English, our children didn't speak the language. It was hard to get the spirit of a new religion in a new country. Finally, after two years of studying with the missionaries, we gained a better understanding of its principles and the story of the Restoration. We prayed sincerely, asking for our Heavenly Father's help. We began to feel a special spirit, something we had not felt before. We know now that it was the witness of the Holy Ghost given to those who seek to know the truth. We finally knew that the LDS Church was, indeed, the right one, and we were baptized.

We had wonderful home teachers—a missionary couple who taught us many more things about the Church. We felt their strength. They also taught us about Christmas and how to celebrate it.

Our first Christmas as Church members brought new insights and understanding. Christmas took on a new meaning. We had a tree that we decorated together as a family. We had a beautiful book called *The First Christmas,* which had colorful decorations inside—pictures of the angel Gabriel, the three Wise Men, Mary, Joseph, and the Christ Child. As we read the beautiful story, we placed each decoration on the tree, and we enjoyed a greater peace on that Christmas Eve than we had ever known before. We strongly felt the Holy Spirit and an appreciation of the Savior.

On Christmas Day, however, I learned a lesson I will never forget. My four-year-old daughter, Dasha, came into the room where the Christmas tree stood. She came to sit on my lap, and as she looked at the tree with the many gifts we had placed under it, she said, "This is so unfair."

"What do you mean, unfair?" I asked.

"This is Jesus Christ's birthday, and we are getting all the presents. What are we going to give to Him?"

She was right. She was just a little child, but she understood the true spirit of the season. It was a celebration of our Savior's birth. I explained to her that when we show love to each other, we are also giving a gift to Jesus Christ.

Yet, her remark stayed with me, and from then on, we decided to add a few more traditions to our celebration of Christmas. Each year we try to do things that show our love for each other and our love for Jesus. We often perform baptisms for the dead at Christmastime. This brings a renewal of the spirit of our Savior's mission. We look for Christmas decorations that will remind us of the true meaning of Christmas. On a separate, small Christmas tree—a gift from the Relief Society—we place a scripture every day during the month of December until Christmas Eve. We read the scriptures together because they help us think and talk about Jesus.

Our first dismal Christmas in the United States is now a distant memory. How different our Christmases are now that we have the gospel in our lives. We know where the joy is found, and it has become a sacred celebration for our family.

We appreciate our membership in Jesus Christ's Church. We are grateful for the spiritual witness that led to our conversion. We recognize that we receive many gifts from our Savior all through the year. We will always try to remember that Jesus is our spiritual master and try to show our gratitude to Him, especially at Christmas.

Helen Glissmeyer has published hundreds of articles in a variety of newspapers and magazines, including Church publications. Author of two books, she lives in Holladay, Utah, where she writes a monthly column for her ward newsletter. She enjoys her children, grandchildren, and great-grandchildren.

*My Spirit shall be
in your hearts, and mine angels round
about you, to bear you up.*

—D&C 84:88

Running the River

by Juliet Emmer

We were six college girls nearing the end of spring semester at the University of Utah, and we planned to run the Yampa and Green Rivers. My best friend, Shirley, and I were roommates, and we looked forward to having a great time together.

For me, it was a daring idea to plan a river-running adventure; I'm not a thrill seeker. And besides, I had just finished a water-safety and life-saving class that I had cursed constantly all semester. I had felt compelled to take it, and it was such a burden to add the hours of pool time to my already heavy college schedule. And I was irritated to discover that there were swimming tests in the pool and written tests on the information in the water-safety and life-saving textbook. So there I was in the water every Wednesday evening and in classes taking additional written exams. I didn't expect to have to work so hard. But it was now spring—time for a little vacation. The six of us would have a great outdoor adventure.

As we set off, we didn't have a care in the world, except for our upcoming final exams. We were going to have fun hiking to see petroglyphs and testing our mettle on the river. Our guides said it would be a pretty routine river trip, except the spring water runoff might make the river run higher and faster than normal. We didn't need to worry, though. With our experienced guides, we would be fine—even if we were city girls—for our May river trip. There would be three rafts, and each one would carry one guide and two girls.

In high spirits, we stowed our gear in the rafts and shoved off. We were all wearing life jackets, and we had been given instructions for making it through the rapids if we were unexpectedly dipped into the drink. Our guides told us, "Go feet first down the rapids for greater safety." Okay, feet first, a life jacket, and a big raft, what could happen?

We could see big boulders on the sides of the river, the swirls of foaming water around exposed rocks, and we could hear the sound of the roaring water. We had been on the river for maybe ten minutes when the raft Shirley and I were in suddenly hit something that bounced the raft straight up and over. In seconds, all of our food, gear, clothing, and warm, dry sleeping bags spun into the rushing water. We were thrown beneath our overturned boat, and I found myself going down, the current pulling me under. I had no idea what had happened to the others, including Shirley, in the swirling, swift current as I was dragged ever deeper under the water.

I fought hard, but I wasn't able to come up to the surface. In fact, I found myself squatting on the river bed. I couldn't get up or get out of the swirling undertow no matter how hard I struggled. It's hard to understand how some things registered so clearly at such a time, but I began to look at my surroundings. The rocks on the bottom of the river were bobbing up and down—it seemed perfectly pleasant to watch them swaying in the current in varying sizes and colors: rusty red with white spots, a light tan color with speckles of glittering gold, or all white, and bouncing off the river bottom. Then I noticed shafts of sunlight that made the water appear to sparkle and shine in several pools of light.

It was enchanting, and it finally occurred to me that I might not make it up to the top. *I am going to die here,* I thought, *and it is so beautiful, peaceful, and lovely. It is a perfect place to spend my last moments.* I wasn't afraid or desperate; I was so grateful that I was in such an ethereal spot.

Almost immediately after thinking I would die and that it was perfectly acceptable, I found myself on top of the water! I looked around in amazement and tried to get my bearings. My troubles were not over. I quickly saw that I was still getting swept along with the overwhelming current. In a sudden panic, I looked for our raft or the shoreline. I began to paddle furiously, but the current was strong, and I realized I was heading straight for a rock wall that went into a pitch-black cave. I frantically tried to swim out of the pull of the water and toward the shore, but I made no progress. I was drifting closer and closer to the rock wall, flailing my arms relentlessly in the fast running water.

Suddenly into my mind came the image of an open page from my water-safety and life-saving textbook with a bold heading at the top: "How to Swim Out of a Current." I certainly did not consciously remember reading it, yet there it was. I "saw" the page with the example of a swimmer and words that explained, "When trying to swim out of a current, let the current carry you as you swim diagonally to the safety of the shore."

I did exactly what my book suggested, and I finally made it to the shore. Much to my relief, Shirley had made it, too. In fact, all the members of our river-rafting party were gathered there in varying degrees of shock. We were shivering and wondering what to do next. Our guides were trying to retrieve our dripping wet gear as it floated down the river.

The trip, which had started in such high spirits, had taken an unexpected turn. The other rafters had stopped to wait for all of us to get reorganized. Shirley, now wearing only one tennis shoe, would not get back into the boat. We were finally assigned to a new guide and a different boat.

There were quiet kindnesses done for us as a result of our trauma. Our former guide gallantly offered us his dry sleeping bag for the duration of the trip, and Shirley and I slept together in his warm bag because our waterlogged bags never did dry out.

I have often reflected with wonder on the river experience. Since that time I have come to realize that I was not alone at the bottom of the river that day. My life was preserved through help from unseen hands as I instantly bobbed right to the top of the water and then was "shown" the exact pages of instruction I would need to get safely out of the swift current and back to shore.

I won't forget the relief I felt when I saw the exact action I needed to take spelled out for me on the pages of that book, and I felt a deep sense of gratitude for every minute of instruction in the class about which I had so frequently complained. My class on water safety and life saving may not have saved any lives but my own, but I am grateful for it now.

I feel a great swell of gratitude to my Father in Heaven, who not only saved my life but also brought to my remembrance the things I needed that day. Shirley and I still talk about those sunbright days with our friends on the Yampa and Green Rivers as we try to sift out the details of the overturned raft.

Since that time on the river, I have not been afraid of death. I know that it can be sweet. There was a calm reassurance that distilled upon me at that moment and an awareness of the simple beauties of life that has never left me. I have an appreciation for everything—the difficulties as well as the victories, the trials as well as the triumphs. I wouldn't change one moment of that day on the Yampa and Green Rivers.

Juliet Emmer, a graduate of the University of Utah in English and sociology, lives with her husband, Paul, in Salt Lake City, Utah. They have four children. She loves to write and served as chapter president of the League of Utah Writers for three years. She enjoys serving in the Church and has held positions in all the auxiliaries.

About the Author

Judy C. Olsen, who graduated from Brigham Young University in 1970 with a B. S. from the College of Family Living, began writing while living in Las Vegas, Nevada, when her children were young. Her first novel, *Dive Into Danger,* a story for young people, was published in 1979. From there she began writing short stories and articles, many of which were published in LDS magazines.

In 1992, Judy and her family moved to Utah. Sister Olsen spent several years as an editor for the *Ensign* magazine, where she wrote and edited articles on marriage and family issues, among other assignments.

In 2007, Sister Olsen's latest novel, *Beyond the Horizon,* was published. The book garnered a Golden Quill award from the League of Utah Writers and was a finalist for the Whitney Award.

Today, Sister Olsen continues to write books with strong family themes, where courage and faith guide the characters' lives and decisions. She also continues to do freelance writing and editing through her website: *www.olseneditorial.com.* Fans are welcome to contact her through her site.

She is married to Donald L. Olsen, and they are the parents of four children and fifteen grandchildren.

If you have a personal, unpublished, uplifting story similar to those that appear in this book, you may contact the author at *judyedits@gmail.com.*